AT A SERVICE NEAR YOU

At A Service Near You

Ruth Gledhill

Hodder & Stoughton
LONDON SYDNEY AUCKLAND

Dedication: To my angel

British Library Cataloguing in Publication Data
A record for this book is available from the British Library

ISBN 0 340 64236 X

Typeset by Hewer Text Composition Services, Edinburgh
Printed and bound in Great Britain by Cox & Wyman Ltd,
Reading, Berks

Hodder and Stoughton Ltd
A Division of Hodder Headline PLC
338 Euston Road
London NW1 3BH

Contents

Foreword

by the Dean of St Paul's, the Very Rev. Dr Eric Evans

During the last few years Ruth Gledhill has, week by week, been making a visit to churches throughout the length and breadth of the United Kingdom. She has actually visited nearly 200 places, and her reflections on each visit have been published most weeks in the Saturday edition of *The Times*. This little book is a compilation of more than sixty of the early visits. This is not intended as an ecclesiastical version of the *Good Pub Guide* but it could well be something comparable. Yet Ruth is not simply a church crawler.

Although she comments on the buildings themselves, she is much more interested in what goes on in them, the people who serve them and the people who find help spiritually by attending them. She is gifted with a great ability to observe and her comments are always charitable. She realises that clergy and ministers and the lay people responsible for our churches have no easy task in today's world and, unlike a lot of modern writers, she looks for the best and emphasises that rather than criticising the worse.

Ruth has done a remarkable job and covered an amazing amount of ground. Worship is the life blood of the Church and her knowledge of the Christian Church at worship in so many different places, modes and varieties of liturgy has given her experience of Christian worship in all its richness which many of us would envy. The book says as much about her as it does about the churches she visits. It is refreshing today to have a critic who is on the side of the angels!

Eric Evans,
Dean of St Paul's

Introduction

This book began life as a column in *The Times*, entitled 'At Your Service', intended from the start to be an innovative look at the depth and breadth of the country's religious life. A number of people deserve credit for the original idea which had been suggested to me by a colleague more than a year before as a 'good sermon guide'. The idea took on a life of its own, as good ones always do, and I was able with help from Jane Owen, the editor of the Saturday *Weekend* section, where it found a home on page two, to develop it into its current shape.

When Peter Stothard became editor of *The Times*, I presented him with a long memo detailing proposed changes to our religious coverage, sticking 'At Your Service' on the end in what felt like a brave but hopeless gesture. He had the imagination to give the column a chance, and there ended my Sunday of rest for the forseeable future.

From the start, the response from readers was almost universally positive. I began with the preconceptions about worship inevitable to one who has experienced little between the extremes of weekly parish church worship at one end, and the splendour and ceremony of State and General Synod worship at the other. Growing up with a clergyman for a father, with childhood memories of church in Essex, Jamaica and Barbados, helped a little although this instilled in me a love for the 1662 Book of Common Prayer which has left me unassailably prejudiced against the banality of the 1980 Alternative Service Book. I decided which churches to visit by word of mouth, personal recommendation and invitation.

'At Your Service' is not on a par with a restaurant guide, despite the occasional criticism that it is irreverently close to such a model, and I always let clergy and ministers know when I want to visit. I refuse to intrude where I am not wanted. Only one place has turned me down. Their arguments for doing so must remain private, but their refusal illustrates the difficulty the modern Church is having straddling the divide between a 2,000-year-old religion and the demands of a market-orientated society, between the conflicting demands of the secular and the sacred. In vain have I argued that

St Paul went into the market place as well as religious places to argue (Acts 17: 17).

Inevitably the column is subjective, and cannot thus claim to be a 'good church guide'. The book cannot cover the country comprehensively, although I have tried to cover as wide an area as possible, straying out of London on many occasions. I began it as a churchgoing Anglican, with fairly traditionalist views. The experience has made me more liberal in belief, and more open to evangelical styles of worship, in particular the joy and movement that come with some of the best spiritual songs.

The book also reflects ecclesiastical news events taking place at the time of my visit, such as the debate on and subsequent ordinations of women priests in the Church of England. As all our religious leaders tell us, we live in a fragmented society. But it has become clear to me, largely through the process of writing this column, that places of worship represent at least one area where a sense of community has not only survived but is growing stronger.

In an age where village, town and city communities are vanishing due to commuting, divorce and changing patterns of leisure, I have become convinced that the churches can and do provide a vital focus for new and growing communities of their own. It is clear that they are valued as places where members can pray, meditate, let go in song and praise and spiritually centre themselves in order to face the pressures, whether familial or material, of the week ahead.

The best churches are those where faith is not used as a liturgical salve, a means of plastering over the cracks, but is given as a foundation on which healing and happiness can be built. Church today seems to be one of the few places where people feel genuinely safe, content and happy. And, when silence is used properly, especially in the older buildings with thick, stone walls, they are one of the few places where it is possible to escape the endless, enervating noise of traffic, telephones and interpersonal anger that permeates daily life.

Ecclesiastical buildings, new as well as old, can have a sense of life and spirituality beyond that created merely by architecture or decoration. In these buildings I have found God where I did not expect Him, and He has felt strangely absent where He should have been present in some.

Friends often pity me this task of visiting a different place of worship each week, a service which has to be fitted around a five-day-week for the home news department of *The Times*. They pity me because they think church is boring, but it can never be dull if you go to a new one each week. The people I admire are those who sit through the same services in the same church every week, the vergers, churchwardens and lay ministers who serve a community which is often small and diminishing with a kind of selfless devotion rarely seen outside the church. Theirs can be a thankless task, and few receive the accolades heaped on those who give their time free to charity. On the contrary, it remains fashionable to mock and criticise those who hold fast to a religious belief, and service in a church, particularly churches where worshippers might be divided over issues such as where the altar should go, and indeed whether it should be called an 'altar' or a 'table', can be as much of a burden as a joy.

The columns are published here without their 'star ratings', a feature of the column about which there is understandably some ambivalence in the churches. Certainly, some places I visited earlier would receive more and others fewer stars in the light of experience. At first I was grateful even to be offered a cup of tea rather than a mere handshake or a polite nod for After–Service Care. Now I would hope for decent coffee or tea, and a biscuit at least. I thank God that I've yet to encounter a church which offers UHT rather than fresh milk.

St Andrew's Parish Church
ALFRISTON
East Sussex
BN26 5TL
(Tel: 01323 870376)

RECTOR: The Rev. Frank Fox-Wilson.

ARCHITECTURE: Begun in 1360 in the form of a Greek cross, St Andrew's is one of the finest flint churches in England.

SERMON: Raymond Woodhams, a Church of England reader and electrical engineer, read his sermon from notes. His modest delivery style almost concealed the best insights, such as on the love of a father for his son, 'the kind of love which is so deep it hurts'.

MUSIC: A relief to let the choir do nearly all the work at evensong after a hard day's walking on the South Downs.

LITURGY: Taken from the 1662 Book of Common Prayer.

AFTER-SERVICE CARE. Badly needed cups of hot coffee served up at the back of the church.

SPIRITUAL HIGH: A church imbued with an ancient joy.

The graceful spire of the fourteenth-century church of St Andrew's rose through the mist like a beacon of hope as we trudged through the pouring rain, wet almost beyond belief.

Peering through my glasses darkly I could just make out the Long Man of Wilmington on the north side of Wilmington Hill, a 226-foot giant who at one time was resplendent with all his manhood but who is now sadly lacking as a result of Victorian 'restoration'. Thankfully, the village church, known as 'the Cathedral of the Downs', suffered no comparable castration during that era of ecclesiastical despoilation. It survives on the Tye, or green, as one of the few old churches in England which was built all at one time and endured no later additions.

The peal of six bells, rung from the floor at the crossing of the cruciform church, called me in to this refuge from the storm. Shaking with cold, and jacket dripping with rain, I encountered not even a raised eyebrow from the immaculately groomed congregation, but was greeted with a friendly handshake and prayer book by churchwardens John Learmouth and Fred Claridge.

The church has about 35,000 visitors a year, and the new rector, Frank Fox-Wilson, has introduced a sung evensong once a month throughout the summer. A table piled high with coffee cups promised warmth to come, even though the pink table cloth beneath them fluttered in the prevailing draughts and the candlelight flickered on the 100-year-old French satin altar frontal, embroidered by nuns at Wantage.

Mr Fox-Wilson had anticipated about two pews full of worshippers, a slight increase on the eight who normally turn up on Sunday evening, but about sixty people turned up and the church seemed packed. For the first hymn, 'Alleluia, Alleluia', the congregation, which included local Roman Catholics and members of the United Reformed Church, sounded faintly uncertain. But the blue-robed choir led us bravely, and gave an impressive rendition of the 'Magnificat'.

Mr Fox-Wilson, in black cassock, white surplice and black preaching scarf, welcomed us all. 'It is a great joy to be together for this first of a series of monthly evensong services during the summer,' he said, as the unsummery wind whistled even more loudly outside. 'I hope you can stay for refreshments before you head out afterwards into this joyful weather.' According to local legend, the original plan was to build the church to the west of the village, but each night after the blocks of stone were transported to the site, some supernatural agency hurled them back over the houses to the Tye, where four oxen were seen, seated with their rumps together. This was taken as a sign that the church should be built there, in the cruciform plan.

'Thanks be unto thee, O Christ, because thou hast overcome death and opened up the gates of eternal life,' said the rector. 'Thanks be to thee because when two or three are gathered in thy name, thou art here in the midst of us.' We prayed for those in grief and peril. We asked for deliverance from 'weariness and continuing struggles, from despondency, failure and disappointment'. Finding ample material for meditation in this, and some consolation in the final hymn, 'The Day of Resurrection', I left in search of a less spiritual and ultimately finite form of refreshment at the fourteenth-century George Inn nearby.

SUNDAY SERVICES: Holy Communion 8 a.m.; family service, parish communion; matins, 10.30 a.m., evensong first Sunday of the month, said service every other Sunday, 4 p.m. in winter, 6 p.m. in summer.

Eglwys Annibynnol Bangor
(the Congregational Church in Bangor), High Street
BANGOR
North Wales
(Tel: 01248 364483)

MINISTER: Parchedig (Rev.) John Gwilym Jones.

ARCHITECTURE: Built in 1881 in the classical or Italian style from Penmaenmawr stone, dressed with Anglesey limestone.

SERMON: Learned exposition that related ancient Bible stories to modern dilemmas over the nature of success and failure, delivered without a text.

MUSIC: Powerful and well-trained voices lifted my spirits, if not the roof.

LITURGY: Nothing used apart from the Bible and hymn book. *LLyfr Gwasanaeth*, the Congregational service handbook, is used for funerals, weddings and christenings.

AFTER-SERVICE CARE: Quick instruction in Welsh language and lore.

SPIRITUAL HIGH: The service was less elevating than calming, but pleasurable nonetheless.

Next to the Harp Inn, the dark grey stone chapel emerged into Bangor's sunlit high street like a living outcrop of the Welsh mountains behind.

Legendary tales of the poetic ability of the new Archdruid of Wales, who preaches there, are spreading fast through the principality. English is his second language, and he cannot help but speak it musically, as if reciting Shakespeare. Even to a non-Welsh speaker, his prayers and sermon in his native Welsh sound like poetry.

John Gwilym Jones was president of the 51,000 Welsh Congregationalists and their 620 churches. He had also been enthroned as Archdruid of the National Eisteddfod of Wales, one of Europe's largest cultural festivals. He led the Gorsedd of Bards, the inner court of Welsh poets, who conduct the prize-giving ceremonies at the eisteddfod. Although Gorsedd members are known as druids, there is no connection between their ceremonies and druidism as a religion.   As a child in Dyfed, Mr Gwilym Jones was steeped in *Y Pethe* 'the things', which embrace religion, writing, music, art and a love of native land. He represents that combination of Celtic spirituality and Christianity that has influenced much Welsh nonconformism, and has done much to preserve the Welsh language from extinction. More than one in four of the population in Wales speaks Welsh, considered to be one of the oldest living languages in northern Europe. A recent survey has shown a slight increase in the use of Welsh among young people. Mr Gwilym Jones says 'The church generally has played a very significant part in keeping Welsh alive. When education in Wales was predominantly in English, church education in Sunday Schools was wholly Welsh.'

Before the service began, the minister and three of his twelve deacons prayed in the deacons' room and then entered through a side door and into the *Sêt Fawr*, a large pew beneath the pulpit. Mr Gwilym Jones climbed into the pulpit, a remarkable mahogany edifice with carved oak panels depicting biblical scenes. We used the new 1988 Welsh Bible, the first new translation to commemorate the 400th anniversary of the Bishop Morgan's 1588 Bible.

The organist, Morfudd Phillips (also one of the leading harpists in Wales), led us into the first hymn. Nothing had prepared me for the gusto with which the hymns were sung, in four parts or more. Mr Gwilym Jones spoke in a soft, poetic but penetrating voice, and led us in prayers *o'r frest* (from the breast). This was the opposite of the nonconformist stereotype of thundering, Calvinist preaching.

'Guide us through the service,' he said. 'We thank you for the unseen fellowship of other churches at worship, and the fellowship through the spirit of those members who are unable to be among us this morning. Help us to search our own hearts during this prayer.' Afterwards, he asked: 'Are there any verses?', at which three children, including two brothers, moved to the front and recited Bible verses from memory.

The minister then spoke in English, to welcome me and the photographer. 'I do not apologise that the service is in Welsh,' he said. 'As we live our lives in Welsh, so also we worship in Welsh.' And to our mutual surprise, both of us were honoured with a public blessing from the minister, a rare event in the life of any journalist, and so far unique in the life of this one.

SUNDAY SERVICES: *Oedfa'r Bore* (morning service) 10 a.m.; *Ysgol Sul* (Sunday School) 11 a.m.; *Oedfa'r hwyr* (evening service) 5.30 p.m.

L'Arche, 'Little Ewell'
BARFRESTON, near Dover
Kent
CT15 7JJ
(Tel: 01304 830930)

RESOURCES CO-ORDINATOR: Maggie Smith.

ARCHITECTURE: Georgian rectory in the Kent countryside, modernised to meet the needs of the community.

MUSIC: Unaccompanied impromptu hymn and chant.

LITURGY: Improvised house prayers after supper, but the community has an international reputation for its liturgies on special festivals.

AFTER-SERVICE CARE: Delicious supper beforehand.

SPIRITUAL HIGH: Insight into the difficult world of those with learning disabilities.

Logs crackled in the hearth of the Old Rectory at Barfreston, Kent, as about a dozen members of l'Arche community gathered for their daily prayers before bed. Bill Armstrong, aged seventy, the oldest person present, reminisced about friends who had died. Dean Hewitt, a young man, talked excitedly about the latest developments in *Neighbours*. Bold paintings by community members covered the walls.

I was at the United Kingdom's first l'Arche community, Little Ewell, founded in 1974. There are now others in Inverness, Liverpool, London, Bognor Regis, Brecon and Edinburgh. L'Arche communities are Christian-based houses where people with learning disabilities live and work alongside assistants. As we settled down to pray, Maggie Smith, resources co-ordinator, explained: 'People with learning difficulties can have quite a profound faith in God. They have a gift of simplicity, of perception.' We held hands and said the Lord's Prayer, and heard a reading from St Paul's letter to the Corinthians: 'Love is patient and kind. Love envies no one, is never boastful, never conceited, never rude; love is never selfish.' The reading was followed by a period of silence, out of respect for the non-speaking members of the eighteen-strong community. Ms Smith then led us in unaccompanied song, 'Come and fill our hearts with love, You alone are holy'.

Another silence followed before some participants improvised brief prayers.

We sang a chant, 'Wait for the Lord, His day is near', before more silence and the community's own prayer, written in l'Arche's early days, which ends, 'Oh Lord, grant freedom, fellowship and unity to all your children and welcome everyone into your kingdom.' Founded in 1964 in a small village in northern France by Jean Vanier, a former teacher of moral philosophy, with the help of a Roman Catholic priest, Père Thomas Phillipe, l'Arche communities now number nearly 100 worldwide.

The official l'Arche charter says: 'Because of their disability and because they feel rejected, a wounded person may shock or repel. But given an atmosphere of security, where their latent capacities can develop, they can also radiate simplicity, welcome, joy and peace.' The residents of Little Ewell, now one of four l'Arche houses in Kent, come mainly through social services and word of mouth. The assistants need no prior training, although training is given within the community. People with learning difficulties and assistants live side by side sharing everyday life. Assistants receive board and lodging and about £28 per week pocket money during their first year. Some, both single and married, may decide to make a long term commitment, describing the relationship between themselves and people with a learning disability as having a quality of 'covenant'.

The residents, aged between twenty and seventy, include Roman Catholics, Baptists and Anglicans. Most attend their nearest churches on Sundays. The Old Rectory has a small chapel used on special occasions, but for daily prayer residents prefer to meet in their living room. They do a full day's work, on a garden project, which is open to visitors, and in a craft workshop, whose products, such as dried-flower arrangements, are sold in the l'Arche shop, St Radigund's Crafts, in Canterbury.

I left with a striking impression of the vulnerability of the residents at l'Arche. Unlike most of us, they had no power to hide their needs from those around them. Ms Smith described how, at a recent Roman Catholic prayer service, one member of the community stood at the 'wrong' time for the 'peace'. He shook hands with almost everyone there, until the stiff and formal atmosphere relaxed, and turned into one of acceptance and love.

Prayers most evenings. Contact the community for details.

St Mary and St Nicholas Parish Church
Church St, BEAUMARIS
Anglesey, North Wales
(Tel: 01248 811402)

RECTOR: The Rev. Gwyndaf Morris Hughes.

ARCHITECTURE: Well-preserved Early English with later additions.

SERMON: *Ffyrnig*, casual and short.

MUSIC: Powerful pipe organ in need of repair. A small choir of ladies sings most Sundays.

LITURGY: Close resemblance to other Anglican liturgies, with some reliance on the traditional.

AFTER-SERVICE CARE: Brief handshake.

SPIRITUAL HIGH: A relief from isolation in this island place.

As I sat on what appeared to be a stone bench in the porch at St Mary and St Nicholas, Beaumaris, on Anglesey, taking in the heady mix of sun, sea and the sacrament, a lilting Welsh voice behind me warned: 'Mind she doesn't bite.' On closer inspection, my resting place turned out to be an ancient sarcophagus, which had once contained the remains of Joan, daughter of King John and consort of Llewelyn ap Jorwerth, prince of North Wales, who died in 1237. The inscription, recorded in Latin, Welsh and English, admonished me thus: that the stone coffin, 'having been conveyed from the friary of Llanfaes and, alas, used for many years as a horse-watering trough, was rescued from such indignity and placed here for preservation as well as to exact serious meditations on the transitory nature of all sublunary distinctions'.

I had driven through wild Wales, and across the achingly beautiful suspension bridge over the Menai Straits to the island of Anglesey, to hear in the old tongue, *yr hen iaith*, about the devil and God, *y diafol a Duw*. The first surprise in Beaumaris was the lack of rain. The second was my ability to follow the service, even though half was in a language I did not understand. We used *The Book of Common Prayer for use in The Church in Wales*, which those who are currently revising the liturgy of the Church of England would do well to examine.

Sensibly, the communion service begins on page one, saving me the usual five minutes trying to find my place after another minute trying to find the index. The liturgy is modern but retains enough of the old-style Anglican prayer book to keep most traditionalists happy. The service is printed with Welsh and English side by side. After a bright 'good morning' in Welsh and English, we sang 'Hark the Herald Angels Sing' in Welsh from the Bangor diocesan hymn book, *Emynau'r Llan*, and said the Creed and the Lord's Prayer in English. The eucharistic prayer was in Welsh and the intercessionary prayers were in a combination of the two languages. The sermon, to my relief, was in English.

Although the church in Wales is Anglican, visitors would be advised never to refer to it as the Church of England in Wales as this will seriously offend Welsh Anglicans. Equally offensive to all other Welshmen, who might be chapel, Roman Catholic or have no religious allegiance at all, is to call it the Church of Wales.

The parish is one of about 600 incumbencies in Wales, which is itself one of twenty-eight provinces or self-governing churches in the worldwide Anglican communion. The church in Wales was created in 1920 after disestablishment and partial disendowment by the Welsh Church Acts of 1914 and 1920. There are more than 108,000 Easter communicants, out of a population of about 2.86 million. Many Welsh Anglicans, and retired Englishmen living in Wales, argue that disestablishment has given the church in Wales a life and spiritual vigour sometimes lacking in its sister church in England.

Apart from the language difficulty (although fewer than one-third of the congregation are Welsh-speaking), and the glimmer of monkish Celtic humour, which occasionally sparkled through the rector's high and dry exterior, I found little difference between this church and thousands like it in the English countryside. The eight bells, six of which were donated by the last Viscount Bulkeley, rang out through the crisp, clear air over the straits towards the mainland, calling the faithful to worship. The rector, Gwyndaf Morris Hughes, a tall, rosy-cheeked figure straight out of a Tolkien novel, wore a chasuble over a white cassock alb, indicating his traditionalist approach. He did not enter the pulpit to preach but strode around at the head of the aisle, catching and holding eye contact to ensure we listened properly to his sermon on the feast of St John the Evangelist.

This was just after Christmas, and just in case anyone was thanking God that Christmas was over for another year, he began: 'We remind ourselves that Christmas starts here on Christmas eve, not about two months beforehand.' Mr Hughes has a reputation locally as a powerful preacher, and he did not disappoint. As with news stories, sermons are nearly always best if brief and to the point, and this was no exception. He noted the conflicting images on television screens over Christmas, with news about starvation in Somalia slotted next to consumer success stories, such as increased car sales. 'What we have this time is a tremendous emphasis on the homeless, the heart-tugging stories that get people into the mood for Christmas. And then we forget it.'

Even the story of Christ in the manger had been turned into 'sentimental smush'. Mr Hughes said: 'If there is a devil, I am sure he is laughing his head off because he has managed to make us degrade this greatest reality in the history of the world.' The church, near the ruins of one of King Edward I of England's fourteen great castles in or on the borders of north Wales, dates from the early fourteenth century. Thousands of holiday-makers pass through each summer, but in the December mid-winter there were few visitors.

In this idyllic setting, it was a passing temptation to forget momentarily the troubles of the wider world. The leaflets at the back, offering advice to parents of drug abusers, and suggestions from Christian Aid on how to save the earth, set near a box for contributions to cancer research, were a chastening reminder that, however beautiful and remote, this church operates in a society which is by no means immune from the kind of problems too often associated only with inner cities.

SUNDAY SERVICES: first and third Sundays, sung eucharist 11 a.m.; evensong 5 p.m.; second and fourth Sundays, eucharist 8 a.m.; sung matins 11 a.m. The Cell, a parish theological discussion group, meets in the vestry on Monday evenings.

Hall Green Preparative Meeting of the Society of Friends
c/o 57 Formans Road
Sparkhill
BIRMINGHAM
B11 3AR

LEADERSHIP: Four elders give spiritual oversight; six overseers
help with pastoral care.
ARCHITECTURE: Built as a reading room in the late nineteenth
century and taken over by the Quakers in the mid-1920s.
SERMON: A talk on children.
LITURGY: No creeds, hymns or set prayer, but there are
readings from Advices and Queries, part of the Quaker Books
of Discipline, which can direct the form of worship.
AFTER-SERVICE CARE: Tea, biscuits, chat.
SPIRITUAL HIGH: More notable for invoking a calm and
peaceful state than for elevating through argument.

I had been told there would be no liturgy or music at this meeting
of the Society of Friends, commonly known as Quakers, five miles
from Birmingham's city centre. There would be nobody who could
accurately be described as minister, vicar, pastor or even leader.
Quite possibly, nothing at all would be said. It presented quite a
challenge.

Entering the red-brick Hall Green meeting house, with its
exposed wooden rafters, wooden floor, an old piano in the corner,
and plastic seats arranged in a circle, felt like stepping back in
time to a village primary school. The meeting was deemed to have
begun when the first Quaker arrived and sat down at about 10.30
a.m. Silence was maintained in the hall from the beginning. Those
who wished to talk stood in the lobby, but within fifteen minutes
the room was full, with equal numbers of young, middle-aged and
old sitting with heads bowed and eyes closed, contemplating in
silence broken only by the sound of traffic passing on a main road
near by.

Shortly before 11 a.m., an elderly man with glasses and in a
smart suit, a retired headmaster, stood to speak. He had intended
to address the children present but, unusually, none had come. 'I
was going to say to the children that prayer is a very difficult thing.

These are my humble thoughts. I think when we pray, we have to be practical. It is no good praying for a safe journey in our car if the fan belt is on the way out. What is the point of praying to be safe on your bicycle if the brakes are not working?' He finished, and there was silence for a few minutes before another elderly man stood. 'I thank God that Geoff has spoken to us as children,' he said.

'If we speak in a way that children would not understand, then adults will not understand either.' More silence, then a young woman in sandals and scarf stood to speak: 'I find it very encouraging that the disciples had to ask Jesus about prayer. They had him to hand and still did not know what to do.' There was more silence, another speaker, then the end of the meeting was marked by everyone shaking hands. Announcements followed, with a report from the Birmingham 'monthly meeting' on local 'preparative meetings'.

The name 'Quaker' is thought to have come from the trembling evinced sometimes at the meetings founded by George Fox in the mid-seventeenth century. Today's name, the Religious Society of Friends, dates from the late eighteenth century, when the Friends held that consecrated buildings and ordained ministers were irrelevant. Quakers hold a belief in the 'inner light', which shows up the darkness within and prompts towards knowledge and truth. Outwardly, calm reigned at Hall Green but, inwardly, there were thoughts as intense as those at any public meeting. Afterwards, over tea, there was quiet but passionate talk of redundancies at the Quaker central meeting house in London and debate about the society's Christian roots.

Many might question the point of spending up to an hour sitting in silence but spiritually, members relish the opportunity to be quiet in a society where noise is omnipresent. Such a meeting must be one of the few places left where peace and quiet can be found and enjoyed.

SUNDAY MEETINGS: 10.45 a.m.; discussion groups at various times.

Camp Hill Seventh Day Adventists
Stratford Road
Camp Hill
BIRMINGHAM B12 OJP
(Tel: 0121-772 4389)

PASTOR: Lee Wellington.

ARCHITECTURE: Modern red-brick, completed in 1987. Surrounded by roads choked with traffic, but inside, the building is cool and spacious.

SERMON: Everything and more than I expected from a profoundly Protestant church.

MUSIC: The children's choir which sang for us and joined us for the second half of our worship is one of four.

LITURGY: No specific liturgy for the service; communion prayers came directly from the Bible.

AFTER-SERVICE CARE: Elders, deacons and deaconesses provide a valuable service in the local community by visiting the sick, helping people with disabilities with their domestic duties and offering advice and support. Twice weekly the church provides a day care centre inclusive of meal and fellowship. The church youth provide a soup kitchen every Saturday night for Birmingham's homeless.

SPIRITUAL HIGH: Occasional moments of sheer joy.

In a small room, sheltered from the barren Birmingham landscape, Sister Dorrell and I poured warm water into basins, washed each other's feet and wiped them with towels. Sister Dorrell was my guide, and this was the 'service of humility' that always precedes communion at the Seventh Day Adventist church in Camp Hill. Our actions followed those in John 13: 1–15, when Christ washed the feet of his disciples and instructed them to do the same.

As the 400 men and women, mostly of West Indian origin, filed out of the two separate rooms where this ceremony had taken place, each dipped a hand into a 'lucky-dip' basket and pulled out a biblical text. Mine read: 'Acquaint now thyself with Him, and be at peace, thereby good shall come unto thee' (Job 22: 21).

Over the few months preceding this particular service, Adventists must have felt as if they were undergoing the trials of Job.

David Koresh, a former Adventist, claimed his Branch Davidian sect was an offshoot of the church and succeeded in attracting some British Adventists into the cult. Some of them died in the flames that engulfed the Waco compound. Adventists deny any link between themselves and Koresh, and in four hours of non-stop worship at Camp Hill, I failed to detect any of the fanaticism of the Waco sect.

Adventists run their lives by a strict and unquestioning adherence to Scripture and believe that Christ's return is imminent. We met on Saturday morning, not Sunday, because they observe the sabbath from sunset on Friday to sunset on Saturday. They abstain from alcohol or other drugs, and for communion we had non-alcoholic wine. They pay a tithe of gross income, do not eat pork and believe in the Protestant doctrine of salvation through faith alone. Worldwide, the church is growing by 7 per cent a year and now claims more than five million people in 25,000 congregations in 184 countries. In Britain there are more than 18,000 Adventists, and the number is growing steadily.

Our morning's worship had begun with 'sabbath school', a service of song, study and personal witness. As well as a minister and his assistant, the church has twelve elders and large numbers of deacons and deaconesses. Elders are lay leaders of the church, and deacons and deaconesses help with practical matters. The women were active in areas such as Bible study, but the second half of the service, divine worship, was male-led. Women cannot be ordained as ministers, although the issue is under study by the worldwide general conference of the church, which takes place every five years.

After singing from the church hymnal, we broke up into groups of about twenty to study the life of Timothy, as told in Paul's letters. We were urged to emulate the 'caring concern' Paul showed for Timothy on his mission to Ephesus. Next came a testimony from Sister Marjorie, who described a recent mission to 'witness' to people on the streets of a Birmingham suburb. 'A lot of people did want to know something about the Bible,' she said.

After a blessing and a short break, we went on to the divine worship, which this week was communion. After prayers, hymns and a special welcome for all visitors, the pastor, Lee Wellington, preached on Christ as 'not a sorrowful man, but a man of sorrows'. In the manner of many talented preachers, Mr Wellington, a slight, charming man outside the pulpit, seemed to grow several feet in height as he moved from a quiet beginning to a thundering climax. 'Jesus Christ is the basis of and the provider of both our spiritual life and our physical life,' he said. 'His sorrow was not that men injured Him, not that men tried to destroy Him. It was that men destroyed their own lives.' Thoroughly chastened, I went into the service of humility. The simple act of washing another's feet, coming after more than two hours of worship and with another to go, was remarkably effective in easing away stress. I left after communion, which we received in our seats, feeling that not only my feet had been washed, but that I had been cleansed all over, freshened up to begin another week after the seventh day had ended.

WEEKLY SERVICES: Bible study hour, 9.30 a.m. Saturday; divine worship, 11.15 a.m. Saturday; youth meeting, 4 p.m. Saturday; prayer meeting, 7.30 p.m. Wednesday.

PROVOST: The Very Rev. Paul Chavasse.

ARCHITECTURE: Renaissance style. Arguably one of the most beautiful churches in the British Isles.

SERMON: Positive reasons given for why God was not trying to make life difficult for us.

MUSIC: Mixed choir regularly sings works by Palestrina, Byrd, Mozart, Haydn and Schubert from organ gallery.

LITURGY: Sung Latin high mass which emerged from the second Vatican Council in the 1960s.

AFTER-SERVICE CARE: Tea and coffee.

SPIRITUAL HIGH: Straddling England's *via media*, almost as holy in its heights and as praiseworthy in its depths as it is possible to be.

The extraordinary beauty of the Oratory was equalled only by the sublime elegance of the ritual employed for this well-attended Latin mass. The drab, cold day encircling us outside was transfigured inside by a golden light, this Birmingham city centre church transformed by Italian marble, mosaic and sensational music into a Roman basilica.

A bell rang from deep within the walls and a procession of priests in gold and purple vestments and their surpliced acolytes were led through the Corinthian columns into the nave by a small boy. Philip Hayward, the thurifer, creating clouds of heady incense. The trinity of priests reached the sanctuary and bowed and kissed the altar in perfect unity. Two clergy elevated the chasuble of the chief celebrant as he censed the altar, and then once more they turned in unison and stood to one side, hands together and heads bowed in prayer. The priest faced us for the greeting, 'Dominus vobiscum', and we responded, 'Et cum spiritu tuo'. We said the confession and we sat while the choir stood in the marble and alabaster gallery above us to sing the 'Kyrie eleison'.

The community of the Oratory was established in Rome during

the Counter-Reformation by St Philip Neri (1515–1595). It was revived in the nineteenth century by John Henry Newman, who founded the Oratorian congregation in Birmingham in 1848 and a second in London, now the Brompton Oratory, the following year. A third was recently founded in Oxford.

Prayer and music are the foundations on which the Oratory is built. Written in red and gold, behind the high altar is the motto 'Domus mea Domus Orationis vocabitur', or 'My House shall be called a House of Prayer', from Isaiah. The first reading, in English, from the book of Exodus, was by Brother Edmund, a former Anglican clergyman. He is one of several more recent converts to Catholicism at the Oratory. Numbers have been swelled by the Church of England's decision to ordain women priests.

The congregation, from small children to fragile elderly couples, appeared outwardly dowdy in comparison to the splendour of the building. But their devotions seemed enthusiastic. During the 'peace' I shook hands with the man behind me, saying: 'Peace be with you.' With a cheeky smile, he responded: 'And with you, kid.' The provost, Fr Paul Chavasse, ascended the alabaster stairs of the pure white marble pulpit, based on that in St Mark's, Venice, to preach on the reading from Exodus. He said: 'When we think of the Ten Commandments, we might ask why did Almighty God establish his law in that way.' It was 'not because God wished to make life difficult for us but because God loves us'. He continued: 'The law of God was established as a covenant between ourselves and our creator, so that we might learn how to act in the way most conducive to true humility.' We said the bidding prayers, prayed for the faithful departed and to the 'immaculate mother of God' as we moved into the Hail Mary. There were two collections, one for the church and one for a charitable cause. The ritual became more elaborate as we went into the eucharistic prayer of praise and thanksgiving, the high point of the liturgy. The three priests stood in line on the sanctuary steps, facing the altar, clouds of incense billowing forth.

As an Anglican, not allowed to receive communion in a Catholic church, I asked for a blessing.

Afterwards the priests proceeded out in silence, leaving me feeling bereaved, as if, in Newman's words, 'I have loved love long since, and lost awhile'.

LATIN MASS: 10 a.m.; seven masses on Sunday, and one on Saturday evening.

St Christopher's Parish Church
Hawes Side
Hawes Side Lane
BLACKPOOL FY4 5AH
(Tel: 01253 697937)

VICAR: The Rev. Graham Rainford.

ARCHITECTURE: Effective modern design by Francis Roberts of Preston. Bare red-brick walls, the only adornment being carved wooden stations of the cross.

SERMON: Impassioned preaching by Fr Rainford. He spoke about vocation, confirmation, meeting his wife and recent events in the life of the church. 'The powerful explosion of God's spirit on this church is what we pray for day in, day out,' he said.

MUSIC: A robed choir sang from the organ loft, with brisk organ accompaniment.

LITURGY: Modern Anglican liturgy.

AFTER-SERVICE CARE: Instant coffee with fresh cream cakes and biscuits.

SPIRITUAL HIGH: A welcome spiritual respite.

The Rev. Graham Rainford, or Fr Graham as he prefers to be known, has a reputation in high church circles that extends south even below Watford. In Blackpool, although the famous lights are not yet switched on, I had expected a display of traditional and exotic Anglo-Catholicism, with incense, bells and ornate vestments.

Instead, St Christopher's was the essence of modern Catholicism within the Church of England. Fr Graham opposed women priests, but had a nun, Sister Mary Jo, as deacon, who was later ordained priest, in 1994, and is now licensed to serve in her own home parish of St Margaret of Antioch, St Anne's on Sea.

He uses the most modern authorised liturgy available, Rite A from the Alternative Service Book, but he attached the 'Regina Caeli' to the end. Bells were rung and candles could be lit beneath a statue of the Virgin and Child, and each year a growing number of parishioners trek off to Walsingham in Norfolk. But little else distinguished St Christopher's from a standard northern Anglican parish church.

As so often, however, appearances were deceptive. Inside the rather bland, red-brick modern exterior, which then lacked even a notice board to identify it as a church, there is a fast-growing parish community which defies those categories and labels by which journalists love to standardise the exceptional. Sister Mary Jo, who took a leading role in the service, was not the only surprise. At a time when the image of the Church is of decline, this parish is proud to declare itself new, founded because there were not enough churches to serve the number who wanted to worship. Over coffee after the service, one member of the parochial church council discussed future events in distinctly evangelical terms, the opposite end of the Anglican spectrum to that practised in St Christopher's.

Blackpool is a town in peril on the sea and in urgent need of salvation, he believed, describing plans for future 'prayer walks' through Blackpool, spiritually to 'cleanse' the town centre. He and others are concerned at the extent of the drunkenness and loutish behaviour which must have been evident to any visitor to Blackpool that weekend. 'Blackpool needs prayer walks,' he stated. 'The Baptists have been doing it for years. It is claiming the territory for Jesus. The people of God in the area are getting to grips with the spiritual warfare being fought.' I arrived for the 10 a.m. sung eucharist, to be welcomed by churchwardens Dave Curtis and Roland Jackson, two 'Brown Owls' preparing to take their Brownies on a pack holiday, PC Pete Webster, the local bobby, and a series of friendly parishioners eager to meet someone who might have been a newcomer to the quiet residential area around us. We were not far from the seafront, or from the wild bank-holiday excesses in this Brighton of the north, but we could have been in a suburb of any civilised provincial town.

The parish was formed in 1989, at a time when it was more usual for parishes to merge with their neighbours and after decades of falling congregations nationwide. For many years before that, a congregation worshipped in a forty-year-old prefabricated building on the same site. Fr Graham has built numbers up to more than 100 each Sunday, in a parish of 8,500. The church building was completed and consecrated two years ago, and the youth club has planted the freshly dug earth next to the red-brick and tarmac, where the new green shoots seemed genuine.

The service followed the usual Anglican pattern of readings, hymns, sermon, prayers, communion and more hymns. We used

the *New English Hymnal*, did one hymn from *Themesongs*, more
often used by evangelicals, and sang the Gospel acclamations in
Latin. We prayed for the Queen and all in government, that 'God
might save all nations from the lust of power and racial hatred, and
that tyranny might crumble'. After communion, a dozen children
came in from their Sunday school for a blessing, carrying paper
doves they had made.

The service lasted ninety minutes, but none complained. Fr
Graham said: 'I have yet to find anywhere that says you have
to worship God in sixty minutes flat. If you are Orthodox it takes
three hours, and nobody says anything about that.'

Despite the freezing British summer outside, the church was
warm. And the simple, unadorned worship was a lesson to those
who seek symbolism in the smallest things. Asked if there was any
significance in the absence of a church notice board, the vicar's
wife, Val, explained it had simply blown down in the wind, and
a new one was being built at that very moment. That new notice
board has been in place for some months now, and displays clearly
the times of worship.

SUNDAY SERVICES: eucharist 8.30 a.m.; sung eucharist 10
a.m.

St Michael's, BRAY
Berkshire
SL6 2AB
(Tel: 01628 21527)

VICAR: The Rev. George Repath.

ARCHITECTURE: Built in Early English and perpendicular styles with tower added later, and extensive nineteenth-century reconstructions in Bath stone.

SERMON: Read skilfully from notes, with inspired moments.

MUSIC: Typical parish church, with organ and *Hymns Ancient and Modern Revised*.

LITURGY: Mr Repath does his best with the material available in the Alternative Service Book, currently being revised.

AFTER-SERVICE CARE: Excellent, with tea and coffee made according to individual need, and opportunity for debate about women priests with lively woman deacon.

SPIRITUAL HIGH: At once high and low, Catholic and reformed.

In his vicarage overlooking the Thames, the present Vicar of Bray, the Rev. George Repath, has the famous ballad about his notorious predecessor pinned over his study desk:

> *In Good King Charles'*
> *golden days,*
> *When loyalty no harm*
> *meant,*
> *A zealous High Churchman*
> *was I*
> *And so I got preferment.*
> *To teach my flock I never*
> *missed,*
> *Kings were by God*
> *appointed,*
> *And damn'd are those that*
> *do resist*
> *Or touch the Lord's*
> *anointed.*

For this law I will maintain
Until my dying day, sir,
Whatever King in England
reign
I'll be the vicar of Bray, sir.

St Michael's, the incarnation of a traditional English country parish church, has as its present incumbent a man who embodies the traditional view of an English country vicar today. If uncertain times returned, he would never need to change the colour of his cloth, because like the church he belongs to, he is already both Catholic and reformed in almost every respect. He is also one of the few vicars to have asked me back to Sunday lunch, an invitation I sadly had to refuse.

With the eight bells ringing out still, I was greeted at the southern porch of the early fourteenth-century flint and hard chalk church by the vicar's wife, Mary, verger, churchwarden and sidesmen. Graham Goy, deputy churchwarden, was clothed in a white cassock alb and amice, a form of embroidered collar. The reason for this impressively clerical dress became clear when, in his alternative role as server, he offered me the chalice during communion.

We used the Alternative Service Book, but Rite B, the more traditional rite, as opposed to the widely disliked Rite A. For stalwart traditionalists, the Book of Common Prayer can be enjoyed at 8 a.m. communion and evensong.

As the service began, the vicar processed from the vestry wearing the full eucharistic vestments, a chasuble over a cassock alb, signifying his Anglo-Catholic roots. I was slightly surprised when a woman, the Rev. Julie Ramsbottom, whose daughter Sarah sang in the choir, then led us in the 'ministry of the word', the confession and other parts of the service, and even more surprised to read in the parish newsletter that Mr Repath greeted with 'great joy' the General Synod decision to ordain women priests.

As the service progressed, the Catholic and reformed elements of Mr Repath's ministry continued to complement each other, a useful example perhaps of how some Anglo-Catholics could gracefully accept the ministry of women priests ordained in the Church of England.

More than 150 people were in church on this second Sunday after Christmas, a day when most would not expect high attendances. Out of a church electoral roll of 197, about 180 normally show for parish communion. The service was intimate and friendly, but we did not shake hands or exchange any physical sign at the 'peace'.

A black and gold notice board near the entrance lists vicars of Bray from Reinbald in 1081, mentioned in the Domesday Book, to the present day. Debate is still continuing over which vicar of Bray was the turncoat of the ballad, thought to have been written by a foot soldier. Symon Symonds (1523–1547) and Simon Aleyn (d. 1565) are the chief contenders, but Mr Repath has established himself as an authority on the subject, and his researches show the original culprit might not have been vicar in Bray at all, but a turncoat Welsh bishop, or a sixteenth-century vicar in Norfolk, Andrew Perne.

In spite of the strong lead set by the choir, the singing took a while to warm up. But by the time we reached 'Hail to the Lord's Anointed' the congregation, of the cheerful and resilient type of men and women who make up the backbone of middle England and home-counties commuterland, was in full voice.

Bray has an audio loop system for the hard of hearing, and microphones and speakers for 'sound reinforcement', although I still had to listen hard at the back to hear what was going on. A service sheet helpfully listed the page numbers as the service progressed.

Mr Repath preached at the chancel steps and not from the pulpit, in order to be closer to those he is speaking to, he explained afterwards. He based his sermon on the day's Gospel, which describes how Jesus stayed behind in the temple in Jerusalem when his parents started for home in Nazareth after Passover festivities. Mr Repath referred to modern biblical criticism, which queries the literal truth of the text. He said:

We have to be aware of the danger of being more concerned with externals than with the truth that is conveyed. What matters most is not whether Jesus was left behind in Jerusalem, nor whether he went with Joseph and Mary when he was twelve. What matters most is what was taking place in Jesus' mind and in his spiritual development. He made use of every opportunity open to him to learn. He discerned between good and evil. He started like the rest of us from nowhere. Where did all this happen? Within the family, both the immediate family and the extended family.

Mr Repath added: 'Our Christian work and duty are to let the childhood pattern be our adult pattern, too. Here where we live, in our homes, in our schools, in our places of worship, in this corner of our world, which is God's world really, that we may be more and more transformed to his likeness and his glory.' As Mrs Repath supplied me with four cups of hot tea in quick succession after the service, the glow of familial pastoral care warmed the ends of my freezing fingertips, while the wintry sun battled hopelessly against the frost on the ground outside, and the Church of England did not seem so unlike God after all.

St Michael's is the parish church of Bray, Braywick, Braywood, Fifield, Holyport, Moneyrow Green, Oakley Green, Stud Green and Touchen-end.

SUNDAY SERVICES: Holy Communion 8 a.m.; parish communion 10 a.m. with Sunday School in term time and crèche in parish hall; evensong 6.30 p.m. Clergy available in homes on Wednesday, 6.30–7.30 p.m.

St Bartholomew's Church
Ann Street
BRIGHTON
(Tel: 01273 620491)

VICAR: The Rev. Vickery House.

ARCHITECTURE: Uncompromising brick structure devoid of spire, tower, aisles or transepts, built 1872. Fascinating in its sheer grandiosity.

SERMON: The Rev. Marcus Riggs, temporarily in charge of the church which was awaiting the arrival of Fr House, preached on the decade of evangelism, now almost half completed. 'I suspect that the majority so far has not even noticed it,' he said. 'We live in a world of empty words. We are bombarded with words, on television, radio, in papers and books. Words, words, words and nothing changes.'

MUSIC: More than competent amateur choir directed by organist Derek Barnes performed Mozart's *Missa Longa* from their substantial repertoire of forty Mozart, Schubert, Haydn, Beethoven, Byrd and Palestrina Masses.

LITURGY: Combination of the English missal, which emerged from the nineteenth-century high church movement, and the widely used, but never fully authorised, 1928 Anglican Series One.

AFTER-SERVICE CARE: No coffee or tea, but invitation to resplendent lunch in nearby Rottingdean.

SPIRITUAL HIGH: Up on a plane of its own.

St Bartholomew's, named after a martyr who was skinned alive, is not only more Roman than the Romans, but in some respects more Anglican than the Anglicans. At 144 feet high including the cross, it is four feet taller than Westminster Abbey and merits the description of the highest parish church in England in more than just its structural sense.

Sir John Betjeman's description of it as 'the cathedral of what used to be called "The London–Brighton and South Coast Religion" with its incense, ritual, embroidered vestments and lights' still stands.

I was one of about sixty people attending solemn mass while

most Brighton residents were enjoying the summer sunshine on the beach. The enormity of this church dwarfed us as we entered the door below a stone statue of St Bartholomew holding his knife. We were met by Bill Blackshaw, churchwarden and lay subdeacon, a title I had not come across before, who is licensed by the Bishop of Chichester to help administer the chalice and assist during the celebration of the mass. The Rev. Marcus Riggs, 'locum' priest helping during the interregnum pending the induction of the Rev. Vickery House as vicar, described himself as 'radical', interested in liberation and feminist theology. Fr Riggs used to run Open Door, a Chichester diocesan support house for people with HIV. He conceded he was slightly bemused at times by the experience of ministering at this church. Luckily, the service at ninety minutes was long enough to take in the theatrical ritual of the priest, subdeacon and the five boy acolytes, as well as absorb the surrounding splendour. The 45-foot marble baldachino in gold mosaic and mother of pearl, the massive brass candlesticks above the altar, the grey and white Tuscan marble candlesticks, the beaten silver tabernacle door and stone and wood carved stations of the cross inserted into the brick piers were a fit setting for the thunderous Walker organ.

In line with tradition, Fr Riggs faced the altar for much of the service while the acolytes milled around, huge clouds of incense ascending from the censer and disappearing up to the boarded roof. Bells sounded at the altar at the elevation of the host and the chalice, with corresponding chimes from the main church bell. Those who looked behind could see Mr Barnes in the loft at his organ, which he played with one hand and both feet, while the other hand directed his twelve-strong choir.

I had often been warned about long sermons but never, as on this occasion, about the length of the Creed, which lasted twelve minutes, this being the *Missa Longa*. With its ornate ritual, elaborate vestments and ceremony, a service here could easily be mistaken for a cross between a concert, opera and play.

But the overall effect made my mind at least more receptive than usual to the sermon and readings, and in particular the line from the epistle of St James: 'If any man among you seem to be religious, and bridleth not his tongue, but deceiveth his own heart, this man's religion is vain.'

SUNDAY SERVICES: high mass with sermon 11 a.m.

St Mary Redcliffe
Redcliffe Way
BRISTOL
BS1 6SP
(Tel: 0117–929 1487)

VICAR: The Rev. Tony Whatmough.

ARCHITECTURE: Medieval church in English perpendicular style, built mainly between 1315 and 1470 on remains of a Saxon building from 789. Famous for the beautiful Victorian spire, surrounded by ornately carved pinnacles.

SERMON: The Rev. Graham Ward, chaplain and fellow of Exeter College, Oxford, compared the first ordinations of women priests to the Easter story. 'Lent has only just begun but already there are signs of resurrection,' he said.

MUSIC: Traditional choir of men and boys only gave exquisite rendition of 'Kyrie' from Byrd's three-part mass for three voices, with main music from the Hereford Service by Richard Lloyd.

LITURGY: Rite B, the better of the two modern communion services in the Alternative Service Book.

AFTER-SERVICE CARE: Good quality instant coffee, tea and biscuits in the undercroft, with friendly chat.

SPIRITUAL HIGH: Extraordinary sense of elation by being in a church named after the mother of Christ on Mothering Sunday for one of the first communion services celebrated by a woman in England.

A church described by Queen Elizabeth I in 1574 as 'the goodliest, fairest and most famous parish church in England' seemed an appropriate place to witness a woman break bread and end the 450-year-old tradition of a male-only priesthood in the Church of England. Of the thirty-two women ordained priest at Bristol Cathedral in the spring of 1994, two were from St Mary Redcliffe.

At our service the newly ordained Jane Hayward, a qualified nurse, was allowed to consecrate the sacrament, break bread, elevate the chalice and pronounce the general blessing at the end. The Rev. Clare Pipe-Wolferstan, a non-stipendiary minister, would celebrate later. At this service at least, the fears of traditionalists that women priests would be the prelude to a radical feminist agenda seemed unfounded. We used the more traditional communion Rite B from the 1980 Alternative Service Book, and *The English Hymnal*.

The service, with elements of ritual more usual in the Anglo-Catholic wing of the Church of England, was a convincing synthesis of old and new. After the initial shock at hearing the clear, soprano tones of a woman's voice pronouncing the eucharistic prayer, the meaning of the words became pre-eminent, the sex of the celebrant irrelevant.

Nearly every seat was taken. Tony Whatmough, vicar, announced: 'This is a normal Sunday service. At the same time of course it is slightly special.' We began with Charles Wesley's moving hymn 'Love Divine, All Loves Excelling', during which a verger, two servers and the choir processed up the aisle, past Victorian oak-doored pews packed with well-wishers. At the rear, with priestly dignity, walked the Rev. Jane Hayward, dressed according to high church tradition in a stylish cream unbleached linen chasuble over a white cassock alb.

She turned to face us, spread her arms wide and announced: 'The Lord be with you.' The strength of the response, 'and with thy spirit', resounded through the columns and ornate vaulting. Yellow daffodils marked this day as Mothering Sunday, while the colours of the stained glass suggested a sunlit day outside quite in contrast to the wind and drizzle.

Geoffrey Robinson, a stained-glass artist and regular member of the congregation, said prayers, remembering 'Jane and Clare celebrating their first eucharist' as well as those upset by the change and 'alienated from the Church that they have known and loved'.

As we moved into the eucharistic prayer, Ms Hayward sang parts of the liturgy, her unaccompanied voice as pure as a choirboy's. But it was as we moved further into the prayer that the meaning of words themselves became, for me, a surprising and unexpected validation of the decision to ordain women.

Afterwards, Hazel Cripps and Valerie Lee, stalwart women of the kind that for decades have been the backbone of the Church of England, celebrated with tea and biscuits in the undercroft. 'We need more priests,' said Mrs Cripps. 'If the ladies are willing to come forward, why not let them be priests?' Mrs Lee added: 'It was beautifully done by Jane. I think women have the same sense of vocation as men.' Everyone seemed reluctant to leave. Women, men and children stayed hugging, kissing and chatting in the nave, porch and transepts until the last possible moment before matins began, savouring their first experience of the ministry of a woman priest.

SUNDAY SERVICES: Holy Communion 8 a.m.; sung eucharist 9.30 a.m.; choral matins 11.15 a.m.; choral evensong 6.30 p.m.

St John's College Chapel
St John's Street
CAMBRIDGE
CB2 1TP
(Tel: 01223 338600)

DEAN: The Rev. Andrew Macintosh.

ARCHITECTURE: A stunning nineteenth-century building in Gothic style, influenced by the Sainte Chapelle in Paris.

SERMON: Canon Stephen Platten, then a member of the Archbishop of Canterbury's staff, gave a meditative homily on creativity.

MUSIC: Perfect but not overwhelming as a complement to the liturgy from a superb choir of men and boys.

LITURGY: Satisfying, poetic and traditional evensong from the Church of England Book of Common Prayer.

SPIRITUAL HIGH: Immensely satisfying.

~

In Cambridge, it is said that those who wish to hear a great concert in an ecclesiastical setting go to King's College Chapel, while those who want worship with great music go to St John's. The chapel choir at St John's is renowed for its Advent carol service, evensong on Ash Wednesday, and its tradition of singing a carol from the top of the college tower on Ascension day. St John's was the first to introduce this form of Advent service in the 1950s; it is now used in most cathedrals in this country and far beyond.

For our service, the sixteen boy choristers and twelve choral students were seated in their stalls, and every seat in the chapel was taken. The choir, directed by the organist, Christopher Robinson, formerly of the Queen's chapel of St George at Windsor Castle, has a strong following in Cambridge. Many worshippers had no obvious link with the university or academic life, but regularly attend services at St John's to enjoy a spiritual and oracular feast. Others there included members of the college, by tradition wearing white surplices.

Seated next to the quire, among the families of the choristers and organ scholars, I found the sound was sensational. 'And the cherubic host, in thousand quires/Touch their immortal harps of golden wires,' they sang, from John Milton's 'Blest Pair of

Sirens', set to music by Sir Hubert Parry. 'That we on earth with undiscording voice/May rightly answer that melodious noise.' The members of the congregation, including my neighbour, Gay Walker, the mother of junior organ scholar Allan, had remarkably melodious voices, as was apparent in the hymns which began and rounded off the service.

In line with 400 years of tradition, the choir, followed by the dean, the Rev. Andrew Macintosh, and the chaplain, the Rev. George Bush, processed from the entrance at the west end through the nave to the quire before the apsed east end of the chapel.

The chapel organ was then being rebuilt, and the congregation launched into the first hymn. 'My God, how wonderful thou art', accompanied by organ scholar James Martin on a Japanese instrument, its huge speakers concealed behind the altar. The effect was electrifying.

St John's has had a choir since the 1670s, and it has achieved a worldwide reputation through recitals, broadcasts and records.

Although walking through the heavily turreted great gate into the first of three courts felt like stepping into ancient history, St John's is not an old foundation, compared to other Cambridge colleges. It is a Renaissance rather than a medieval body, and has acquired a reputation for scientific and mathematical achievement as well as theology.

The present chapel, built in 1866-69 by the architect Sir George Gilbert Scott, replaced the chapel of the thirteenth-century hospital which originally stood on the site. Evensong is sung six days a week during term, with sung eucharist on Sunday mornings. The choristers attend St John's school at the western edge of the college, which has 420 boy and girl pupils.

Even the spoken parts of our service had musical intonations, the rhythmic phraseology of the 1662 Book of Common Prayer perfectly at home beneath the Gothic-style arches and the wooden roof intricately decorated with Christian figures through the centuries.

The choristers, in traditional red and white, sat quietly throughout the two lessons, from Jeremiah and St Paul's letter to the Hebrews, urgent messages to each other being passed only through what appeared to be a discreet sign language. In between, in magnificent style, they rendered a perfect 'Magnificat', and topped the lessons off with the 'Nunc Dimittis'.

After the Creed, the Lord's Prayer and three brief prayers, collects for the day, for peace and for help, the choir sang the anthem and we moved into the sermon. Canon Stephen Platten, the guest preacher, was at the time the Archbishop of Canterbury's secretary for ecumenical affairs. He spoke from a stall at the west end of the chapel, an almost indistinguishable speck in the distance, but every word was clearly audible. Aware of the imminence of Christmas, he spoke of divine and human creativity, the need for mystery and human greed, the 'root cause of sin'.

After prayers and a hymn, members of the college went to dine in hall and the rest of us headed for home. After such a celebration, further nourishment, spiritual or temporal, seemed unnecessary.

SUNDAY SERVICES: term time only, sung eucharist 10.30 a.m.; evensong 6.30 p.m.

Eglise Protestante Française de Cantorbéry
Chapelle du Prince Noir
Canterbury Cathedral Crypt
CANTERBURY
CT1 2EH
(Tel: 01227 456676)

PASTEUR: Dr Hugh Boudin.

ARCHITECTURE: The Black Prince's chantry, stylishly adapted with Victorian fittings, is a hidden gem among the Gothic arches of the crypt.

SERMON: Plea for a rediscovery of the faith and conviction that inspired the Reformation.

MUSIC: Expert organ-playing from Dennis Matthew, whose ancestors imported powder puffs from France.

LITURGY: Worship of God in the language of love, a service of the word undimmed by Protestant puritanism.

AFTER-SERVICE CARE: Tea, cakes and chat in a nearby cafe, reputed to have been a weaver's house, an industry influenced by Walloon and Huguenot refugees.

SPIRITUAL HIGH: A step into an enclave of charm and hospitality.

Undefeated by the drizzle, huddles of teenage French boys defiantly eyed the local girls on a street corner in Canterbury while before them, unrecognised, passed the proud descendants of Protestant Walloons from the Low Countries and Huguenots, on their way to church. Tourists strolled by without a glance, and possibly only those looking for it noticed the small sign near the entrance to the south transept of Canterbury cathedral indicating the French Protestant church in the Black Prince's chantry.

The Protestant Walloons and Huguenots fled to Britain from the Spanish Netherlands and France during the religious persecutions of the sixteen and seventeen centuries; less than 2 per cent of the French population is now Protestant.

After descending the winding, wooden staircase into the crypt, I entered a dim, cosy refuge, where a persecuted past seems contained but not forgotten. At the entrance is an arresting portrait of Admiral Gaspard de Coligny, the leader of the Protestants killed in France during the 1572 massacre of St Bartholomew's day; his brother, Odet, a Roman Catholic cardinal, is entombed in the cathedral above.

The pulpit stands in the centre, in front of two banks of pews, while behind it, half veiled by a blue velvet curtain, a large Dutch landscape depicts the arrival of the Protestant refugees in England about 400 years ago.

Members of the French church have been meeting in the mother church of the worldwide Anglican communion since Queen Elizabeth I gave them the crypt in the sixteenth century, and I had expected that the ensuing centuries would have Anglicised this church. The dismay I felt on learning that the entire service was to be in French was surpassed only by my surprise that, with my A-level tutoring, I could understand it, once I stopped confusing the French word for sin, *péché*, with that for peach, *pêche*.

The congregation included a number of tall, blond aristocratic descendants of the original refugees, such as Michael Peters, secretary of the consistory, the equivalent of the church council. My neighbour was a moustachioed, twinkly-eyed man of military bearing, Alexander Lamaison, who mysteriously described himself as a 'retired government official'.

At one time, nearly one-third the population of Canterbury was of French or Flemish descent. Many Kent and Sussex families can trace Huguenot or Walloon ancestry. Although numbers have declined, the church is experiencing something of a renaissance, and every seat was taken at our service. For this, the members credit Pasteur Hugh Boudin, a former professor of Protestant theology in Brussels, who is fluent in five languages and arrived here in 1991. Wearing a black Geneva gown, preacher's scarf and white bands, he conducted the entire service from his pulpit. His accent, when we spoke (in English) later, was unplaceable, a product of his birth in Auchterderran, Scotland, to a Scottish mother and Belgian father. His wife, Anna-Birgitta, is Swedish.

The service was in modern French, and followed an order similar to that in a Presbyterian or Congregational church, with many hymns and chants interspersed with Bible readings, prayers and the sermon. Nearly all the hymns were psalms, a tradition of Huguenot worship. Many well-known English hymn tunes, such as the Old Hundredth and the Doxology, originated in the French psalter.

We proceeded with commendable pace through the *ordre du culte*, arriving quickly at the prayers and the sermon, when Pasteur Boudin examined some of the reasoning which inspired

the Reformation, and asked where those passions were today.
'We must be faithful to the sacred text,' he said, and warned
against the tendency of some Protestants to elevate Scripture to
the point almost of idolatry. 'The last authority does not rest in
the Bible, but in the Lord.' As we left the crypt, cold and damp
had defeated the winter sun. But I will not forget this corner of
Canterbury that is forever France.

SUNDAY SERVICE: 3 p.m.

The Cathedral Church of the Holy Trinity
CHICHESTER
West Sussex
PO19 1PX
(Tel: 01243 782595)

DEAN: The Very Rev. John Treadgold.

ARCHITECTURE: Small and intimate by the standards of most cathedrals. Romanesque in style, mostly completed by 1123. The original fifteenth-century spire collapsed in 1861 but was rebuilt immediately afterwards.

SERMON: Bold and, at times, contentious address from the jovial Bishop Michael Marshall, the Archbishop of Canterbury's adviser on evangelism.

MUSIC: Fabulous performance of Haydn's *Missa Sancti Nicolai* with men and boys' choir accompanied by small orchestra.

LITURGY: Rite B from the Anglican Alternative Service Book, a serviceable cross between the more modern Rite A and the 1662 Book of Common Prayer.

AFTER-SERVICE CARE: Coffee served in the Bell Rooms, the cathedral refectory in the cloisters.

SPIRITUAL HIGH: Enlightening encounter with the artistic elite of Sussex.

As with so much in Sussex, Chichester Cathedral entices from the outside, but working out how to get in presents something of a problem. Having wandered around the cloisters in search of an entry sign I finally found a way in through the west door to be warmly greeted by the stewards and vergers handing out the *New English Hymnal* and service sheets. Almost every seat was taken by a congregation which included the actress Patricia Routledge and Sir Philip Ward, the Lord Lieutenant of West Sussex. More than two-thirds of the 400 people there were regular attenders.

This was the service to mark the beginning of the city's twentieth annual arts festival, which initially celebrated the 900th anniversary of the foundation of the cathedral. Celebrated by the dean, the Very Rev. John Treadgold, the 11 a.m. festival eucharist was without question one of the finest performances of all. Seated near the front with Paul Rogerson, the festival's artistic director, and Lianne Jarrett, also involved in organisation. I was in a good position to witness the colourful procession of the choir in deep red cassocks and white surplices, and the magnificent array presented by the cathedral chapter, who stood motionless and statuesque beneath the Gothic arches of the chancel screen for half of the service, and who at the peace processed to the High Altar Sanctuary for the Ministry of the Sacrament. Behind them could just be made out the bright colours of the 1966 John Piper tapestry hanging in the sanctuary.

'I do hope we are going to have a wonderful two-and-a-half weeks here in Chichester welcoming relatives, friends and many people from a long distance away,' announced the dean after we struggled gamely through a little-known hymn dedicated to the doubting St Thomas, whose feast day it happened to be.

The journey and entire service were made worth while by the performance by choir and orchestra of Haydn's 'Kyrie Eleison', which evoked the pre-Victorian, pre-organ days when string ensembles and orchestras in church were the norm.

Chichester is one of the foremost traditionalist dioceses in the Church of England, where opposition to women priests remains possibly the strongest outside London. Women servers in cassock albs and bearing crosses surrounded the pulpit while Bishop Michael Marshall read the Gospel and launched into his powerful sermon. He advocated the importance of enjoyment, and even made a few jokes, a gambit too rarely deployed by other preachers.

'The Church of God is essentially into the celebration business or it is not in business at all,' he said. 'Everyone from princes, politicians and prelates, and most certainly the General Synod of the Church of England, we all take ourselves far too seriously by half. We have frankly forgotten in the Western world how to enjoy ourselves.' People were created to worship God and to enjoy him, he said.

SUNDAY SERVICES: Holy Communion 8 a.m.; choral matins 10 a.m.; sung eucharist 11 a.m.; sung evensong 3.30 p.m.

St Mary's Church
Bettws Gwerfyl Goch
near CORWEN
Clwyd
LL21 ORU
(Tel: 01490 420313)

DEACON-IN-CHARGE: The Rev. Sally Brush.

ARCHITECTURE: Small medieval church consisting of nave, chancel and sanctuary, packed with beautiful oddities and ornaments, including the only surviving rood of its kind in Britain behind the altar with a relief of Christ and the words 'Ecce Homo', behold the man.

SERMON: Based on a local pilgrimage taking place the following day, which was Rogation Sunday. The pilgrims followed an ancient Celtic route passing through Bettws.

MUSIC: Just two hymns.

LITURGY: Welsh prayer book authorised in 1966 for experimental use by the governing body of the Anglican Church in Wales. Falls half-way between the Church of England's Book of Common Prayer and the 1980 Alternative Service Book.

AFTER-SERVICE CARE: Sally Brush had to rush off to do another service in one of her five other churches, but the congregation is welcoming to newcomers and the church community is active throughout the week.

SPIRITUAL HIGH: Candlelit eucharist performed by a woman for women in twelfth-century church redolent of Celtic legend shed a new light on the dark ages of the Church.

Beneath my feet, the red tiles formed a small bump that seemed to move slightly. This was the resting place or otherwise of Gwerfyl, daughter of Cynan, Lord of Meirionnydd, the eldest illegitimate son of Owain Gwynedd, twelfth-century Prince of North Wales and, according to family legend, one of my own ancestors. The deacon, the Rev. Sally Brush, who, with her frilled dog collar and slight stoop beneath her black cassock, appeared herself to have stepped out of ancient history, explained that the bump was thought to be Gwerfyl trying to get out.

The name of the village, Bettws Gwerfyl Goch, means the

bead or prayer house of Gwerfyl Goch. The last word, from the Welsh *coch* refers to the red colour of her hair. There has been a church on the site for more than 1,300 years. Although originally dedicated to the sixth-century Breton, St Elian, the church was rebuilt by Gwerfyl and like many dedicated to early Celtic saints it was rededicated to the Virgin Mary, who became a cult figure in the Middle Ages.

Given that the congregation was nearly all women, Miss Brush's valiant performance, not only taking the service and preaching but playing the organ also, made opposition to women priests seem somehow odd. Women were not ordained in the church in Wales and for our eucharist, the bread and wine had been consecrated by a male priest in advance. Miss Brush wore her stole over one shoulder instead of round her neck, as a priest may do, and missed out the prayer of consecration in the eucharistic liturgy.

Gwerfyl's church, encircled by a mossy path and uncut grass scattered with dandelions, was one of many threatened with closure in a Church with declining congregations. It was saved by the efforts of its small but devoted band of members. Seated in front of me were Joan Crawley, the vicar's warden, Barbara Bowler, a Methodist lay reader licensed to take services on a rota system and Lizzie Currie, the 'people's' or church warden. Behind me sat Edith Fogg, who described herself as 'general dogsbody', and on the other side of the straw-matted aisle was Elena Williams, the secretary, treasurer and local historian.

In her sermon, Miss Brush referred to the former healing ministry of one of her churches, Ysbyty Ifan, founded in the twelfth century to help care for those injured in the Crusades. As she read an old Welsh poem on charity, 'Copia blawd dy frawd difri gwer eidil', or 'Remember the plight of your poor brother, weak, feeble', I thought not of the Crusades, but of where Gwerfyl's church would be without its women.

SUNDAY SERVICES: second and fourth Sundays 9.30 a.m.; first and third Sundays 2.30 p.m.

Dagenham Parish Church
Church Lane
DAGENHAM
Essex
(Tel: 0181–592 1339)

TEAM RECTOR: The Rev. Mike Reith.
ARCHITECTURE: Charming and cheerful with medieval feel.
SERMON: Determinedly evangelical, strong.
LITURGY: Combination of modern and traditional.
AFTER-SERVICE CARE: Coffee, tea and biscuits after the service with friendly church staff and members.
SPIRITUAL HIGH: Beacon of light in a gloomy place.

Dagenham, in Essex, spiritual birthplace of the Archbishop of Canterbury, Dr George Carey, inspires almost indescribable depression at first sight. Inadequate signposts left me lost in the middle of a run-down housing estate, with a scrawny mongrel the only living creature in sight. Through the graffiti-marked towers I spotted the corner of an oldish-looking building. It turned out to be the old rectory, now the headquarters of a transport company, and one of three remaining old buildings in the centre of Dagenham. The other two are the parish church and the Cross Keys pub next door.

St Peter's and St Paul's, more commonly known as Dagenham Parish Church, must be one of the few historic churches in England not defaced by a bright Christian mural on its tower. In such a loveless landscape the words, 'God so loved the world that he gave his only son', from St John's Gospel, offer much-needed crumbs of comfort. Tired Ford cars, and one Skoda, populated the church car park. I wondered where all the human beings had gone. It turned out they were nearly all in the packed and friendly church. The environment improved audibly when the peal of six bells rang out through the chilly morning air.

Dr Carey is a friend of the rector on my visit, the Rev. Deryck Spratley, and spent much of his early life as a regular church member. Mr Spratley has recently been replaced by the Rev. Mike Reith. The clergy do not robe up any more, and Mr Reith's big concern is to encourage church members to help their friends become Christians too. Moves are afoot to make the area more attractive and Mr Reith hopes the derelict pub next door might become a community centre.

Under his leadership, the church has remained in the traditional evangelical mould which inspired the archbishop. Mr Spratley allowed women church members to lead worship but opposes women priests, citing the New Testament in support of his belief that man is the head of the woman. For the morning service he wore the traditional Anglican vestments of black cassock, white surplice, black preacher's scarf and a blue hood to denote his theological college, Oak Hill in Southgate, north London.

This is the heart of Essex, but I saw not a single example of the much lampooned 'Essex man'. In church I sat next to a beautiful, dark-haired young woman with a labrador at her feet. She explained she had gone totally blind at the age of ten, when her retinas became detached overnight. The church does not specialise in the healing ministry, but there were other sick people there, scattered among the stalwart middle-aged women who make up the bulk of traditional church-going England. The impression, with light streaming through the high arched windows, was of hope and inspiration staying ahead, just, of the surrounding despair.

Unemployment has devastated the congregation, cutting church income drastically. It is clear that the parish is facing serious debts for the first time in its history, which is long. Parts of the church date from the twelfth century, when it was built to cater for the needs of the tenants of Barking Abbey, the local fishermen, woodsmen and farm workers. The church was plundered during the Reformation but survived until the second Sunday in Advent, 1800, when the congregation was waiting in the churchyard for the vicar, who was late. While they were waiting, the tower fell on to the nave and destroyed the roof, porch, gallery and pews. No lives were lost, but everything except the chancel and north chapel had to be rebuilt.

In the Advent that followed the vote to ordain women priests in 1992, a blow comparable in its psychological impact fell on the congregation, when Mr Spratley shared his doubts about women priests. He was still then considering his future as a priest. 'It seems to me such a contradiction of what Scripture says,' he said. 'It is a possibility that I will leave the ministry.'

Mr Spratley was like one of Dickens's benign characters, with a short, grey and silver whiskery beard, and eyes that twinkled behind large glasses. Women regularly lead worship at Dagenham, so his doubts cannot be dismissed as mere chauvinism dressed up as Scripture. Under his leadership, the church strengthened. In a matter-of-fact manner, he announced the remarkable news that the 300 shrubs planted in the graveyard were growing well. In an area where vandalism is endemic, it was worthy of note that so many shrubs had survived, he explained. And while most churches suffer from inadequate heating, the problem at Dagenham is that the electric pipes under the pews are too hot. Careless adults can burn their legs on them and crawling children have been known to burn their heads. A sign announces that the heating is now turned off in the areas where children sit.

As we waited for morning prayer to begin, gospel songs were piped in through an impressive sound system. But for the service we switched to organ accompaniment, apart from a brief interlude from a guitarist. We sang songs from *Mission Praise*, the hymn book compiled for the Billy Graham missions to Britain. In the modern evangelical style one or two worshippers raised their hands in the air, but most were content to sing their hearts out, as if to sing their troubles away.

One such trouble is drug abuse. In 1985, Mr Spratley conducted the funerals of four young men who died as a result of drug abuse, all in the space of six weeks. Two were brothers, and soon he was conducting the funeral of their mother. Made desperate by the horror and extremity of what he saw around him, Mr Spratley founded Daybreak, a drug counselling service, funded by the Church Urban Fund and Barking and Dagenham council. His friend, Dr Carey, agreed to become patron. Mr Spratley believes no human situation is beyond God's power to redeem, and he disagreed that it must be hard work, even for God, in Dagenham. 'There is very little self-esteem. I believe the Christian Gospel is the answer. God loves people. He loves the people around here as much as any.'

In his sermon, a strong testimony, to which the congregation, children included, listened with rapt attention, he spoke of light and faith amid the darkness. 'Maybe there is a time when God cannot be found, but there is never a time when God cannot be trusted,' he said.

SUNDAY SERVICES: Family service 11 a.m., evening worship 6.30 p.m.; plus Holy Communion at 6.30 p.m. first and third Sundays of the month, at 8 a.m. on second Sunday, at 11 a.m. on fourth Sunday and noon on fifth Sunday.

St Nicholas Church
Market Place
DURHAM
DH1 1JP
(Tel: 0191-384 1180)

VICAR: The Rev. Michael Wilcock.

ARCHITECTURE: Elegant Victorian Gothic-style church, with the comforts of a modern evangelical interior.

SERMON: An assumption that Bible stories can be taken as read, and an emphasis on bringing them to life in the present.

MUSIC: Traditional hymns and evangelical songs, with acoustic guitar and piano, or organ.

LITURGY: Imaginative format based on the Alternative Service Book, with modern and non-sexist 'inclusive' language.

AFTER-SERVICE CARE: Coffee, tea and opportunity for personal counselling or prayers for those in need.

SPIRITUAL HIGH: Warmth and friendliness.

Arriving half an hour early for the evening service at St Nicholas in Durham, I was invited by worship leader John Payne (who has since moved on) to join a handful of regular members in 'a time of prayer for the service'. This is a common feature of churches in the evangelical tradition. Dr George Carey, now Archbishop of Canterbury, was vicar here from 1975 to 1982, and the internal arrangement of the building as well as some features of the service date from his incumbency. However, the evangelical tradition of the church dates back at least 150 years.

It is hard to imagine the church as it once was when most services were conducted according to the 1662 Book of Common Prayer, when the building was cold and damp, and hymns were accompanied by the sound of drips from the badly leaking roof. Today, the stiff wooden pews have been replaced by comfortable chairs. A communion table stood on the south side of the church, where the Rev. Michael Wilcock, the preacher, and Mr Payne stood for our service.

In spite of freezing winds outside, the church was blissfully warm. As four of us prayed in the centre of the church for half an hour, the empty, barn-like structure gradually filled with people, mostly students dressed casually in jeans, trainers and warm jackets. The church is so popular that the morning service has been split into two, with about 150 at one and 300 worshippers at the other.

The organist, Imogen Taylor, a maths student, was baptised five years ago. She explained the appeal of St Nicholas: 'It has good preaching, and it is friendly.' The problem with some other churches, she said, was that 'either nobody speaks to you or everybody seems to be bored'.

Jenny Wade, aged eighty-five and a regular member for forty-five years, said: 'This church brings the young people in, and they are the ones who have to carry on when we are gone.' She said that her life had been irrevocably changed by an adopt-a-student scheme introduced by Dr Carey during his time there.

'Students can get very homesick. We have them for tea or coffee once a fortnight.'

After notices of a forthcoming study programme and an invitation to prayers in the chapel later, our service began with a call to repentance. 'If we say we have no sin, we deceive ourselves, and the truth is not in us,' Mr Payne said, leading us to confess that 'we have sinned against You and against other people in thought and word and deed'. We sang the popular song, 'Give Thanks with a Grateful Heart', and were asked to think about the lines, 'And now let the weak say I am strong, let the poor say I am rich, because of what the Lord has done for us.' Preaching and song are central features of services at St Nicholas. Mr Wilcock, working his way through St Mark's Gospel, had reached the end of chapter seven, where Jesus was reported to have healed a deaf mute. 'People who meet Jesus in the stories of Mark's Gospel find Him amazing,' he said.

'The words used to describe the reactions of those who encounter Him are "astonishing", "surprising" and sometimes "terrifying".' The students listened attentively as he explained: 'It is Jesus in whom God has come into this world, who says, I am the one you need, I am the one in charge of the forces of nature, who provides for all these people. Put your trust in the Gospel which is sufficient, not only for you but for all the world.' He led us into prayers, another song and then the Apostles' Creed before the evening collect, intercessionary prayers and spontaneous prayers.

We ended with a thanksgiving and a prayer by John Chrysostum, the eastern saint whose evocative liturgies are being used increasingly in western churches. This prayer of his had long been a basic Prayer Book item. 'Fulfil now, O Lord, the desires and petitions of your servants, as may be most expedient for them,' we prayed.

In *The Church in the Market Place*, Dr Carey described the trials and triumphs of the transformation he worked on St Nicholas. In a later book, *Spiritual Journey*, he reports the views of young people who complain that Anglican church worship consists of 'long lessons, lots of prayers, dull sermons, hymns that drag on and on'. At St Nicholas, these failings seem to be avoided, while valuable elements of traditional worship are preserved.

Anglicans in Durham are praying that Dr Carey will be able to work the same miracle with the Church of England as a whole.

SUNDAY SERVICES: morning service 9.15 and 11 a.m.; evening service 6.30 p.m.; Holy Communion is alternated with Morning Prayer and Evening Prayer.

The Cathedral Church of Christ and Blessed Mary the Virgin
DURHAM
DH1
(Tel: 0191–386 4266)

DEAN: The Very Rev. John Arnold.

ARCHITECTURE: Twelfth-century Romanesque, the finest example of its kind in England. Breathtakingly beautiful.

SERMON: Discursive for matins, exegetical at communion.

MUSIC: The organ was out of action and we heard Beethoven, Brahms and Schubert by pianist Keith Wright, with anthems by Byrd sung by a choir of men and boys, directed by James Lancelot.

LITURGY: The 1662 Book of Common Prayer for matins, with the modern Rite A from the Alternative Service Book for communion.

AFTER-SERVICE CARE: We strolled through the monks' door and the shaded cloisters for coffee in the Prior's Hall, former dining-room of the deanery, and orange juice or sherry after communion.

SPIRITUAL HIGH: Security and vulnerability inspired by the early-Norman fortress feel to the building, and the sensation of being in a house of God reaching heavenwards from its setting by the river Wear.

For those of us expecting the thunderous sounds of an organ, there was a sense of bathos when, instead, we heard the slow movement from Beethoven's 'Pathetique' sonata (Op. 13), played on the piano.

The unexpected beauty of Durham Cathedral, with its icy air, the delicate wooden carvings and cold stone walls, created a curiously intimate atmosphere among those of us seated in the choir. I was in an honorary canon's stall, the best seat in the house after the ornate fourteenth-century Bishop's throne next to it. Opposite and above me were the organ pipes, silent while the console was being rebuilt. We were at matins, with a congregation that was largely middle class and middle-aged, dressed warmly in long, expensive woollen coats and tweeds.

Durham Cathedral was built on the site of the tenth-century

White Church, the shrine of Cuthbert of Lindisfarne, the most popular saint of the North East.

The opening line of Scripture in the enchanting language of the 1662 Book of Common Prayer set the tone for me of the entire morning. 'The sacrifice of God is a troubled spirit: a broken and contrite heart, O God, shalt thou not despise,' read the precentor, David Meakin, from Psalm 51.

Without an accompanying organ, the boys' voices echoed through the vaulting as if from a former age as we progressed through the 'Te Deum' and the 'Jubilate Deo'. In the Creed, we spoke of the Holy Ghost instead of the Holy Spirit, and used the more intimate 'thou' and 'thy' instead of 'you' and 'your' throughout the liturgy. The Archdeacon, the Venerable Derek Hodgson, preached on declining respect for the monarchy, Parliament and other institutions. He said: 'We have seen a walking away, physically, emotionally and mentally, from the great institutions of our national life.' The communion service, about fifteen minutes after the close of matins, was celebrated in the choir, although congregations are increasing to the point where the Dean and Chapter are to move it into the nave. Many undergraduates from Durham University attended the communion services.

The congregations at both included Captain Dick Annand, of the Durham Light Infantry, a holder of the Victoria Cross from 1940, and his wife Shirley. I sat next to Alastair Sharp, a retired circuit judge, and his wife Daphne. Regular members also include Professor Arnold Wolfendale, the Astronomer Royal, and the cathedral Chapter includes the Rev. Margaret Parker, Durham's first woman minor canon.

Over coffee, served between the services, we discussed the Right Rev. Michael Turnbull, who was then about to succeed the controversial David Jenkins as Bishop of Durham. Canon Hodgson said: 'The response has been uniformly positive.' Worshippers were interested in his pastoral style, which they judged good and caring. There were about 150 people at each service; the number doubles during the summer tourist season. The bishop, who preaches on the main festival days, can be relied on to pull in a big crowd.

For communion, I joined those who spilled over into the nave, where we were handed hymn books without the music line, and where even tone-deaf worshippers sang with glorious abandon, enjoying the freedom inspired by the architecture around us. We were led into the liturgy by Ruth Etchells, a member of the General

Synod. There was something extraordinarily beautiful about the clear tones of a woman's voice announcing the hymn, the readings and the psalm.

The Dean, the Very Rev. John Arnold, preached from the quire, delivering his message on New Testament miracles of healing with powerful conviction, his voice at times shaking with passion. He said: 'Nowadays, Christian healers should follow Jesus not so much by copying his words and gestures literally as by using the techniques and knowledge of our day with similar zeal and faith.' To receive communion, we knelt at the high altar in front of the intricate Neville screen, behind which lie the remains of Cuthbert, and above which is suspended a spectacular blue, red and gold tester.

At the end, there was something almost ghostly about the way the Dean and Chapter, then the choir, processed out to the sound of Schubert's 'Impromptu' No. 4 in A flat. Their soft tread became a faint rhythm beneath the music that kept many of us in the congregation transfixed in our seats, haunted by the notes long after the last echoes had died away.

SUNDAY SERVICES: Holy Communion 8 a.m. and 11.15 a.m.; matins 10 a.m.; evensong 3.30 p.m.

The Greyfriars Tolbooth and Highland Kirk
Greyfriars Place
EDINBURGH
EH1 2QQ
(Tel: 0131–225 1900)

INCUMBENT: The Rev. David Beckett (The Rev. Ewen MacLean takes the Gaelic service).

SERMON: in Gaelic.

ARCHITECTURE: Post-Reformation simple Gothic style. No spire or pews. Small belfry installed recently on the north gable.

MUSIC: Wide range of liturgical and choral music at main service, haunting psalms in the Gaelic service.

LITURGY: Structured order at English services, simple and Bible-based for Gaelic.

AFTER-SERVICE CARE: Friendly Scotsmen and women offer plates of excellent buttered scones, biscuits and tea. Active outreach to homeless people.

SPIRITUAL HIGH: A warm shield against the cold outside.

The drinking fountain with a statue of Bobby, the faithful Skye terrier who sat for fourteen years by the grave of his master until his own death in 1872, was scarcely visible through the freezing hail, snow and wind at the corner of Candlemaker Row in Edinburgh. I walked through the Greyfriars church gates, past Bobby's pink granite memorial stone, to be greeted with a cheery, 'go as a cha thu?' Finlay Morrison, a fellow worshipper, wanted to know where I was from. Scotland suddenly seemed a little farther north of Watford Gap than I had imagined.

I was at one of the few weekly Gaelic services in the Scottish lowlands, although Gaelic is only a small part of what happens at Greyfriars. The Gaelic speakers used to have a Highland church of their own, St Columba's near the Usher Hall in Edinburgh. In the late 1940s, they moved to Tolbooth St John's, by the castle, which is now closed. Our service was in the St John chapel, created in the southwest aisle at Greyfriars when the Highland congregation moved again in 1979.

The Rev. John Campbell, who is over eighty and from

Dunfermline, came out of retirement to take the service. The usual minister at the Gaelic services, the Rev. Ewen MacLean, was away. Mr MacLean, a Glasgow-born native Gaelic speaker, was the previous incumbent at Greyfriars.

We sang no hymns. Instead Roderick Macdonald, the precentor, 'precented' the psalms, a Highland tradition which dates from a time when churches did not have musicians and few people were literate. With his beautiful tenor voice, he 'lined out' the Gaelic psalms. This meant singing a descant line which we repeated, with embellishments from the more practised members of the congregation. We began with Psalm 135, to the old Scottish tune of 'Kilmarnock'. As the eerie melody, a cross between Celtic tribal music and Gregorian chant, echoed around the enormous church, it was not difficult to imagine that outside, covered by heavy snow, were bracken and hills around unfathomable lochs.

The church is popular with tourists and students. Ivan Derzhanski, aged twenty-five, from Bulgaria, is in Edinburgh studying for a doctorate in cognitive science. Asked why he was learning Gaelic, he said: 'I am fond of languages in general. Being in Scotland was an opportunity to add another one to the list.' He speaks about eighteen tongues and has progressed to reading lessons in Gaelic. Phonetically, Gaelic most resembles Russian, he said. Unlike Welsh, it was difficult to guess at the pronunciation. Even the Lord's Prayer, from the first line, 'Ar n-Athair a tha air neamh', to 'ghloir' (glory), was hard to follow.

Apart from standing briefly at the beginning and end, we remained seated throughout. With the help of Mr Derzhanski, Phyllis Reoch, a church elder, and *An Tiomnadh Nuadh*, the Gaelic–English New Testament provided, I could follow the New Testament reading, Mark 9: 14–25. The Old Testament reading, from 1 Samuel, about God's problems in communicating with his servant Samuel, I had to guess at.

For his sermon, Mr Campbell took two verses from the New Testament reading as his text. He preached from notes, his hands clasped in front of him, eyes beseeching us to believe for the sake of our salvation. I guessed correctly that he was talking about doubt and faith. Basic comprehension was made possible by his occasional references to Iosa (Jesus), dramatic gestures and mournful expressions. His last parish was Urquhart, on the shores of Loch Ness, where he counted the fabled monster as a member of his congregation.

After the service, most of the fifteen or so worshippers chatted over hot, strong tea and buttered potato scones. There were two MacDonalds, a Morrison, Munro, Greig and MacLean. Unlike many English churches, where women often predominate, here the men outnumbered the women three to one. Sadly, only one, Archibald Macpherson, a law lecturer at Edinburgh's Heriot-Watt University, wore a kilt.

Dr Farquhar Macintosh, former rector of the Edinburgh Royal High School and chairman of the Sabhal Mor Ostaig, a Gaelic college, said the total number of Gaelic speakers had gone down but increasing numbers of youngsters were taking the language up again. Iain Ferguson, who teaches Gaelic at evening classes, mounted a defence of the much-maligned Macbeth. 'He was the last Gaelic-speaking king. He was not a bad king either. He did not die the way Shakespeare said he did.' Greyfriars is part of the Church of Scotland, an established Presbyterian church with a system of courts instead of bishops. The National Covenant, a protest which led to the end of royal control and the episcopal regime, was signed here in 1638 in front of the pulpit.

The seventeenth-century church, the first built in Edinburgh after the Reformation, takes its name from the Franciscan Grey Friars who ministered there from 1447 to 1560. The graveyard in which the church stands was once the Grey Friars' herb garden, given to the town by Mary Queen of Scots in 1562 as a burial ground.

Instrumental music was banished from the Church of Scotland in the seventeenth century and restored for the first time in Greyfriars, when a harmonium and then an organ were installed in the 1860s. The 1850s stained glass at the east end was the first post-Reformation stained glass to be installed in a Church of Scotland church. Greyfriars is one of the few churches in the land which regularly uses psalms in the metrical, Anglican, plainsong, Gelineau and Gaelic versions.

In less inclement weather, the Highland service attracts many Gaelic learners. The kirk minister, the Rev. David Beckett, who does not speak Gaelic, said: 'It does seem to us important that this tradition is maintained. There is a revival of interest in Gaelic language and culture, and we like to think that this forms a centre for people with an interest in things Gaelic.' He sees the task of Greyfriars as building bridges towards Edinburgh University as the university parish church. There are lunchtime services for the commuter population of the parish, and it is also a venue for recitals, concerts and lectures. A team of divinity students works from the church hall, providing meals and entertainment for the city's homeless and disadvantaged, who congregate in the Grassmarket nearby.

SUNDAY SERVICES: parish worship 11 a.m. with crèche, Sunday school, coffee and lunches in Kirk House; Gaelic service 12.30 p.m.; Holy Communion 9.15 a.m. on first Sunday of each month; evening service 6 p.m., second Sunday of each month, Oct-May; early service 9.30 a.m., Sundays mid-June to mid-Sept.

Renfield St Stephen's Church of Scotland
260 Bath St
GLASGOW
G2 4JP
(Tel: 0141–332 4293)

MINISTER: The Rev. David Lunan.

ARCHITECTURE: We met in the 1970 St Matthew's chapel, whose modern style, described by one architect as 'brutal', is ameliorated slightly by the stylish main church building next door, in English Decorated Gothic style.

SERMON: Biblical exposition on the nature of vision from Mr Lunan, plus a debate on the problems of the modern church between him and his associate, the Rev. Keith Steven.

MUSIC: Enjoyable but with piano-led hymns and gospel songs.

LITURGY: Bible-based structure which worked well in this context.

AFTER-SERVICE CARE: Walk though kitchens to a room being redecorated in the neighbouring church centre for tea, biscuits and friendly chat.

SPIRITUAL HIGH: Engendered faith in the power of the Church to overcome darkness.

Renfield St Stephen's, in the heart of a Glasgow red light district, is competing for souls against the more immediate lures of drink, drugs and prostitution. The church, with its elegant steeple rising through the swirling snow against a blackened evening sky, seems to embody the haunting spirit of an age long forgotten.

The Church of Scotland is one of two churches established by law in the UK. Unlike the Church of England, the other established church, the Church of Scotland is separate from the State and does not have the Queen as its supreme governor. The Lord High Commissioner represents the Queen at the church's annual assembly in May. Like the Church of England it is Reformed, but unlike it there is no tradition of bishops or episcopal government. Instead it is a Presbyterian church, regulated by a system of councils, committees and courts.

Protestant churches are by nature evangelical, in that they

emphasise personal salvation, personal conversion and the authority of Scripture. But the Rev. David Lunan led us in an informal-style evangelical worship, unusual north of the border. The hallmarks of this are the extensive use of gospel songs and modern hymns, little or no set liturgy and frequent reference to the living presence of Jesus Christ during the service.

This Scottish congregation was far removed from many English evangelicals, who wave their hands in the air during hymns, clap, shake tambourines and sometimes burst into glossolalia, the ecstatic speaking in tongues associated with the charismatic renewal movement.

After five years, Mr Lunan reports an emerging freedom in his Scottish worshippers, who joined in the hymns with spirit but were otherwise relatively restrained. It was evident during the service that he is slowly leading worshippers towards a more relaxed style.

We used the Good News Bible, with *Mission Praise*, which began life as a song book for the Billy Graham mission to the United Kingdom, and *Songs of God's People*, a Church of Scotland hymn book supplement. We sang more hymns and songs in an hour than I recall having sung at any service in my life, with half a dozen before the service even began.

The atmosphere in St Matthew's chapel was intimate and familiar. Mr Lunan's two young sons, Iain and Malcolm, raced freely around the small, red-velveted interior. His wife Maggie sat with another son, Andrew. Most members of the congregation were young, casually dressed in jeans and sweatshirts. Mr Lunan wore a shirt and sweater, another feature of the freer evangelical style, although he wears a cassock for the morning service in the main church building, which, in keeping with the ornate Gothic interior, is more formal.

When Mr Lunan arrived five years ago, the church had about 580 members. Most were elderly. Numbers have declined to 380, although he is not aware of anyone who has left. The sad fact is, most have simply died. 'It does not trouble me too much because I think my job is to bring in the next generation,' Mr Lunan says. 'There is inevitably a transition period. But I think I can live with that.' At our service numbers were small, about twenty, but 200 turn up most Sunday mornings.

Mr Lunan runs his church by the motto of the city: 'Let Glasgow flourish through the preaching of thy word and praising thy name.' Like the Church of Scotland, Mr Lunan's style is Christian first, Reformed second and Scottish only third. His supreme rule is the Bible. But he calls himself a 'liberal evangelical', with an emphasis on the social message of the Bible as much as on personal salvation.

Almost anyone attending this service, even if they had never been to church, would feel comfortable. There was no sense of exclusion, either in terms of liturgy and song, or of salvation, and there was no collection. 'We do not have an offering but if anyone wants to make a contribution, there is a plate,' Mr Lunan announced.

Prayers, led by the associate minister, Keith Steven, followed a casual evangelical pattern but were evocative and moving. The intense expressions on the young faces around us were suddenly explained. These people believe passionately in the power of their prayers to change themselves and those around them. 'We praise you, O God, that you have called us into the community of your church to share life together, to live life in such a fashion that others will see that we are followers of Jesus because of the quality of love that there is among us,' said Mr Steven.

Although the evening service is sometimes graced with a sermon, on this night we had a question and answer-type debate between Mr Lunan and Mr Steven.

'It is terribly easy for congregations not to look beyond their immediate life, to be so absorbed with what is going on inside their own walls that they fail to see the larger issues,' Mr Steven said. A failure to reach out and engage with fellow Christians 'imperils the life of the church'.

Churches, he said, need to unhook themselves from seeing their ministers as the focal point of life. 'In a reformed church, we try to believe in the priesthood of all believers. We must not lose sight of the raison d'être of the church, to take Christ into the world and to bring people into discipleship of him.' As we chatted in a large room in the chilly centre afterwards, these two ministers seemed suddenly indistinguishable from the ordinary church members, a small but definite sign of hope in the struggle ahead.

SUNDAY SERVICES: morning service 11 a.m., a varied pattern of worship 7 p.m.; the Lord's Supper in October, December, March and June, second Sunday evening each month; plus Wednesday lunchtime service.

Holy Disorder
Christ Church
Brunswick Square
GLOUCESTER GL1
(Tel: 01452 410022)

WORSHIP LEADER: Tim Mason.
ARCHITECTURE: Built in 1822 for visitors to Gloucester spa. The many alterations since make for a bizarre combination of Romanesque and other styles. Has been described as 'exotic and revolting', but is oddly attractive inside, with barrel vault in nave, no pillars and excellent acoustics.
SERMON: Mr Mason discoursed expertly on God's love to a rapt audience.
MUSIC: Keyboard, drums and acoustic guitars led modern hymns to a rock beat. Even the older people danced.
AFTER-SERVICE CARE: None at church, but newcomers are taken into 'care groups' of a dozen people who meet on Saturdays.
SPIRITUAL HIGH: Like a rave, with the Holy Spirit instead of drugs.

In the churchyard of Christ Church, Gloucester, young people were eating sandwiches and hugging in the pink glow of the setting sun. Inside, the church stretched eastward into a gloomy dusk, relieved only by an eerily glowing cross at the back of the sanctuary, the effect of a cunningly placed spotlight. A painting of Christ in the small dome in the apse was lit like an icon. This was Holy Disorder, a lively youth service singled out for special praise at a recent meeting of the General Synod of the Church of England.

The teenagers who crowded into the pews were dressed in faded and torn denims topped by baggy T-shirts and sweaters. As we launched into the first hymn, 'Swing Wide These Gates', I stood with the half-dozen others over thirty years old, in a pew near the back. Our vision was obstructed by our agile neighbours, who, at the first drum beat, leapt on to the wooden pews and began to sing and dance through the three-hour service. Many hymns ended with loud whistles and cheers from the congregation.

In order to see, I was forced to overcome thirty-three years of conditioning and climb on to the seat of my pew, only to find my vision further obscured by 'dry ice', white smoke billowing into the aisle. During the second song, we moved to the words and music. Coloured disco lights flashed, the spotlight on the cross changed from white to red and back to white again, and candles glowed through the mist.

Holy Disorder began in November 1992 in Gloucester with about fifty people and has grown to more than 130. Three similar services have begun near by, bringing attendance to more than 300.

There were few clergy. The service was led by Tim Mason, aged thirty-nine, the diocesan youth officer, who wore sandals, socks and brightly-coloured beads in his hair. After our lively beginning, Mr Mason asked us to sit. Instantly, silence filled the church. 'We just celebrated Jesus's love,' he said. 'Let's just think about that now. If you talk about love in the world, they think of the birds and the bees.

'But love is an important thing. I am learning about love every day, about the hurt that relationships in families create. We never tell people these days we love them in case they get the wrong idea. The message of this service is love.' This was the prelude to Holy Disorder's version of the peace, when most congregations shake hands. 'Let us demonstrate our love for each other,' said Mr Mason. The church erupted into laughter, tears and shouts of joy.

Teenagers leapt over pews, ran up the aisle and hugged each other. I tried to shake hands with my neighbour, who looked shocked. 'You can't do that here,' he said, and gave me a bear hug. The enthusiasm was chaste. The service seemed not an avenue to but a relief from the sexual pressures faced by teenagers.

More songs were followed by workshops. Bible study was in the back room, prayer in the vestry, drama in the churchyard and discussion in the nave. We heard a testimony from Lorna Stephens, aged seventeen, who had been on tour with an orchestra. 'I was on a coach and I was told all Christians were unquestioning, and that being a Christian was a cop-out,' she told the hushed and darkened church. 'I told them it was a cop-out not to be a Christian, because it is easier not to believe what is in the Bible. Every Christian has some doubts, but if you have faith, God gives you the strength to believe.' Mr Mason followed this with a pep talk on being a Christian. 'It was not easy for Jesus. People shouted at him, laughed at him, despised him. But it is worth it because there are so many young people hurting. How many of you know young people taking drugs, drinking and abusing alcohol, stealing, unhappy with life?' Many hands went up. 'Most of the problems young people face are because they feel a lack of love.' There was no lack of love in the church, however. We sat on the floor in the dark, sang slow hymns, prayed and held hands. The lights went on at the end.

'Send us out from here, Lord, with your love and your care. Bring us back next week to celebrate again.' I went out into the darkened streets of Gloucester. On a street corner near by, two women screamed at each other while a baby in a pram looked on in silence. I was glad the teenagers, still discussing God's love in church, did not witness this.

SERVICES: Thursday, 7–10 p.m. at Gloucester; Monday, 7.30–9.30 p.m. at Holy Trinity, Stroud; Tuesday, 7.30–9.30 p.m. St John's, Coleford; Wednesday, 7.30–9.30 p.m. St Mary's, Thornbury, Avon.

High Street Methodist Church,
HARPENDEN
Herts
AL5 2RU
(Tel: 01582 713056)

SUPERINTENDENT MINISTER: The Rev. John Walker.

ARCHITECTURE: Twentieth-century Gothic style, similar to many Anglican parish churches.

SERMON: Rousing and methodical, with thought-provoking social commentary.

MUSIC: Conventional but strong, with enjoyment and involvement a high priority.

LITURGY: Fluid with innovative moments.

AFTER-SERVICE CARE: Few can escape without a word or handshake. Tea and coffee before morning worship and after morning family services. Church open for coffee Mon-Sat, 10 a.m. to noon.

SPIRITUAL HIGH: Impressed by the method in their spirituality.

Apart from the annual Methodist conference, my only previous experience of the Methodist church at prayer was at Wesley's chapel in City Road, London, when Baroness Thatcher was 'in conversation' with the minister, the Rev. Paul Hulme. Asked if she considered herself Methodist or Church of England, she said: 'I was brought up to believe that John Wesley lived and died as a Church of England believer.'

Visitors to the Methodist church in the High Street at Harpenden, Hertfordshire, will favour this view. If Wesley, the co-founder of Methodism, were to be resurrected and make his first pastoral visit to the town, he could be forgiven for believing that Methodism and the Church of England are still one. Many in the congregation were Anglican, and in some senses the church fulfils all of the functions expected of a typical Anglican parish church. Geoff Mainwaring, one of four stewards, said: 'I am an Anglican born and bred but I have been a Methodist twenty-five years. There is not much difference really.'

The Rev. John Walker was recovering from flu. 'I come to you this morning courtesy of Lemsip, antibiotics, sheer, dogged will and the Holy Spirit,' he announced throatily. Even so, his sermon was impressive. He led us in worship with all the Protestant vigour that I had been led to believe was still extant in Methodism.

With a membership of more than 600, his church is one of the two biggest Methodist churches in the country. This was the third Sunday in Advent, and all the children were absent, preparing for their nativity play in an adjacent hall although for much of the service I could hear them in the wings, like distant angels singing from on high. Even so, the church, built in 1930 with seating for 500, was full to capacity. Worshippers were friendly and earnest. Most appeared to take seriously Wesley's injunction to earn, save and give all you can. They included millionaires, leading bank managers, senior civil servants and captains of industry.

The stewards wore name tags, appendages which other churches could usefully copy. I was guided to a pew and handed the Methodist hymn book, *Hymns and Psalms*, the liturgy for morning worship, adapted from the Methodist Service Book, and a Good News Bible. Somewhat unusually, the church has a robed choir, noted as one of the best choirs in Methodism, who led us through a succession of heartily sung, well-known hymns. My neighbours in the chestnut wood pews were enjoying their own singing too much to notice when I hit the odd wrong note.

The High Street church is one of four Methodist churches in Harpenden. Mr Walker heads a circuit of ten churches, which is one of thirty circuits in the London North-West District. A Methodist district is the equivalent of an Anglican diocese, although most cover a larger area. We were celebrating the feast of John the Baptist, the outspoken prophet who was the inspiration for many of the early Methodist church leaders. Mr Walker called us to repentance. Because of his flu, he could not do it as thunderingly as he might have wished, but it was still effective. We reflected contritely on our sins of laziness, vanity and indulgences of the flesh; on habits of falsehood and uncharitable words; on our evil thoughts and lapses from faithful and religious practices. Mr Walker led us in all this while we remained seated, our heads bowed. Earlier, I had been sad to learn that the congregation would not join in saying the confession, though they do so at Holy Communion, but after Mr Walker's admonition I no longer felt the need. As we moved on to say the traditional version of the Lord's Prayer, with the 'thou art', the 'thy' and the 'thine', I began to feel at home. This impression was completed when we joined the choir in the 'Te Deum', to an evocative musical setting

I had not sung since adolescence. The prayers touched a chord: we prayed for the British troops in Bosnia and the US forces in Somalia; for the depressed and 'those who find the prospect of merriment overbearing'; for 'those who want to hide away'; and for the sick. We remembered a girl, aged three, who had collapsed in church the previous Sunday with a stroke.

Like many ministers around Britain, Mr Walker spoke in his sermon of how to celebrate Christmas at a time when so many had nothing to celebrate. 'It is a sombre scene. Redundancy has hit this congregation during the last year. Not a few people have been deeply affected,' he said. His advice was to eschew consumerism and get involved. Many in the congregation were already committed to community life.

'The people of Harpenden have enough about them to be creative non-consumerists,' he said. 'Let's go along the path of John the Baptist. Let's not be afraid to be different.' Wisely, Mr Walker did not dwell on the fate of St John.

SUNDAY SERVICES: Holy Communion, 8 a.m., first Sunday in the month and 9.15 a.m., second Sunday in the month; morning worship, 10.30 a.m. (Holy Communion third Sunday in the month); evening worship, 6.30 p.m. (Holy Communion fourth Sunday in the month); twenty-seven house groups meet regularly. There are three church choirs. Scouts, Guides and women's groups meet in the church.

St Winefride's
Guardians of the Shrine of St Winefride
15 Well St
HOLYWELL
Clwyd
North Wales CH8 7PL
(Tel: 01352 713181)

PRIEST: Father Daniel Lordan.

ARCHITECTURE: Nineteenth-century stone and red-brick church, remodelled in 1912, its pale yellow walls, bare apart from the stations of the cross, evoking the austere spirit of Lent.

HOMILY: Father Lordan urged us to remember that Lent was a time of spiritual renewal, when the church wants us 'to enter into ourselves and find there the God who made us and the God who loves us'.

MUSIC: Combination of traditional and evangelical hymns, with mixed choir of adults.

LITURGY: Standard Roman Catholic service, printed with responses on a mass sheet.

AFTER-SERVICE CARE: Tea and coffee.

SPIRITUAL HIGH: Healing and restorative, if taken in with a visit to the shrine.

The light in the confessional box indicated that Father Lordan was hearing confessions before mass, so we walked round the corner to take the waters at St Winefride's well, one of the 'seven wonders of Wales'.

St Winefride's is the site of an unbroken tradition of Roman Catholic worship, dating back at least to the seventh century, when Winefride, the daughter of a local patrician, was martyred. A virgin soon to become a nun, she resisted the advances of Caradoc, the son of a neighbouring prince, who pursued her and caught her on the threshold of the church. When she resisted, he hacked her head off with his sword. Her uncle, St Beuno, cursed the prince and, according to legend, he died and the ground opened and swallowed him. St Beuno prayed that Winefride's life be restored. The well gushed forth where her head had fallen, and she was restored to life and lived another fifteen years.

The well has been a centre for pilgrimages ever since, even when they were forbidden by the civil authorities after the Reformation. The church stands on the site of the Star Inn, which the Jesuits used as cover until Catholic emancipation last century. It now attracts about 50,000 people a year, although it is little known outside Wales. Until the 1960s, crutches and leg irons of people supposedly cured there lined the back wall of the crypt, beneath the lofty traceries of the Gothic stonework. They were removed because they were thought to be creating the wrong kind of interest in the shrine, known as the Lourdes of Wales.

A spring bubbles in the inviting pool, in the shadow of a beautiful fifteenth-century chapel where pilgrim and occasionally Greek Orthodox services are held. A few coins surround the stone, lying in the pool, on which St Winefride's head was restored to her body when her uncle prayed over her.

Each summer, between Pentecost and the end of September, the Litany of St Winefride, 'Glorious Virgin and Martyr', is said daily at the shrine and worshippers venerate a single relic, her little finger bone, stored in a safe at the church.

The Saturday mass is one of the best attended, and there were about fifty people in church as the sun set over the Welsh hills. Father Lordan urged us to remember the season. 'The austerity of Lent is brought home to us in the lack of decoration and flowers,' he said. 'The signs of austerity are important because we want to be with Jesus in the desert.' He continued: 'Let us become aware of our unworthiness, of all that is disordered and broken in our lives, of all that will separate us from Jesus and one another.'

After the penitential rite and the readings (one done by a woman reader, Thelma Kavanagh) and the homily, Father Lordan asked those of us who were not Catholics and therefore could not receive communion to come to the altar with hands crossed over our chests, as a sign that we wanted a blessing instead.

Afterwards one parishioner, David Schwarz, an optometrist, explained how his family ended up by mistake in this corner of Wales. His grandfather, an unemployed watchmaker from Germany, had thought he was landing at Holyhead when he found himself at Holywell by mistake in 1864. He discovered his mistake, but so liked the waters that he stayed.

WEEKEND MASSES: Saturday 6 p.m.; Sunday 8 a.m. and 10 a.m.

St Thomas Penny Street
LANCASTER
LA1 1XX
(Tel: 01524 62987 or 32134)

VICAR: The Rev. Peter Guinness.
ARCHITECTURE: Gothic revival described as 'Victorian ware-
house' by the vicar.
SERMON: Targeted to a youth audience.
MUSIC: Excellent singing by different music groups, accompanied
by keen musicians.
LITURGY: Accessible.
AFTER-SERVICE CARE: Newcomers receive large doses of
tender loving care.
SPIRITUAL HIGH: Few could leave without believing in some-
thing.

After nearly three hours in church, it was time to wake up. 'The
spirit comes; a wind,' said Brian McConkey, the preacher, catching
me in the middle of a huge yawn. At that moment, a gusting wind
blew up outside, rattling the timbers of this enormous, bleak,
Gothic church, and causing the youngsters around me to shiver
inside their torn denims and shapeless pullovers. Mr McConkey
seized his moment. 'Be aware of the Holy Spirit filling your whole
being, making God real to you,' he declared.

I was in Lancaster, and had escaped from the wind, rain
and gloom through huge, vivid-purple doors into St Thomas
Penny Street, to celebrate Evening Communion and continue
with 'the Late Service', a charismatic evangelical event aimed at
the young.

Much effort had gone into dressing scruffily, as it had into
transforming this dismal church into a receptacle fit to be 'filled
with the Holy Spirit'. If ever there was a 'grunge' church, this
is it. We sat in oak pews which could have used a polish, knelt
on worn brown carpet, were oppressed by whitewashed walls and
yellowing gloss paint on what once must have been attractive plain
wood panelling. Damp patches showed on the ceiling. The finest
features, the stained glass and a carved reredos, were barely visible
beyond a newly plastered chancel wall. 'It's very shoddy,' said the

vicar, the Rev. Peter Guinness. 'The church employs so many people that most of its budget goes on missions and staff.' Mr Guinness hopes to restore the building, but all churches could learn from the temporary improvements effected by the youngsters for their Late Service.

His curate, the Rev. Trevor Mapstone, who preached at the preceding communion, is paid about £12,000 a year; the vicar earns a little more. As with most evangelical churches, the congregation of 370 adults and 150 children takes giving money seriously. Of the £100,000 income, £42,000 goes to the Blackburn diocese. The youth minister's salary comes out of the remainder, which also finances a part-time secretary and cleaners. The coffee-bar manager and assistant are self-financing through the shop. Between 10 and 15 per cent of church income goes to missions and charities.

The church was packed at both services with students from Lancaster University and St Martin's College. Many wore tense expressions, linked to the exams.

After communion, while we sipped coffee, a group of young people transformed the church with ink-dyed muslin drapes, a vast improvement. Big loudspeakers were installed, and the chancel and sanctuary were screened with a colourfully lit white cloth stating 'Welcome'. A saxophonist, guitarists and excellent female vocalists took the floor. The decibel count was lower than usual because the lead guitarist and drummer were camping in the Yorkshire dales.

Colin Phillimore, one of the guitarists, led our worship: 'We are here to party and celebrate the coming of the Holy Spirit; His power in our lives,' he said, leading us into the opening number. 'Jesus, we celebrate your victory'. The youngsters, some in their early teens, began dancing, and a young man in torn jeans and satin waistcoat banged the pew with his fist in time to the music.

The next song was written by the group, which was not highly competent musically but was impressively creative. 'Get ready to ride on the wind of the spirit,' Mr Phillimore announced. His language, typical of the charismatic movement but rare outside it, was as improvised as the songs.

We moved into 'Purify my heart', with many praying on their knees. A woman in orange dungarees walked down the aisle and danced to the music on the chancel steps.

The charismatic movement came to Britain early this century, but since the 1960s has been growing fast in the main Christian denominations, including the Roman Catholic church. Charismatics emphasise the gifts listed in 1 Corinthians: speaking in tongues, prophecy, healing and exorcism. Until recently, speaking in tongues, or glossolalia, has been the most prominent, but this is declining and features briefly in the services at St Thomas; healing and prophecy are becoming the norm.

The church has a healing ministry, including programmes to help people with addictions to anything from drugs to perfection. Church members 'laid hands' on others who knelt for communion during the first service, and none blinked as the curate said during his sermon: 'We are in the last days; Jesus is speaking to us now.' It transpired that he did not mean that the apocalypse was imminent, but was referring to the concept that the 'last days' began from the time of Christ.

But as he continued to speak on the Holy Spirit, with which 'God is saying He's going to drench his people. He's going to soak them', the imagery was made more immediate by the tempest blowing outside around the dark grey stone edifice which shadows the shopping precinct in Lancaster.

SUNDAY SERVICES: 10.30 a.m. and 6.30 p.m. alternating between Morning and Evening Prayer and communion; evening communion followed by the Late Service at 9 p.m.

The Parish Church of St Peter-at-Leeds
KIRKGATE
Leeds
(Tel: 0113 2452036)

RECTOR: The Rev. Stephen Oliver.
VICAR: The Rev. Christopher Cornwell.
ARCHITECTURE: Early Victorian Gothic, seating 2,000.
SERMON: An intelligent tribute to the trials of the unemployed.
MUSIC: Fabulously deep, resonating sounds evocative of monastic
  life from the famous surpliced choir.
LITURGY: The beautiful language of evensong from the 1662
  Book of Common Prayer.
AFTER-SERVICE CARE: Coffee, tea and conversation.
SPIRITUAL HIGH: Almost transcendent sense of light emerging
  out of a Gothic darkness.

The poet, Sir John Betjeman, in a BBC broadcast in the late
1960s, cited a saying in Leeds: 'High Church, Low Church and
Leeds Parish Church'. The church is a sort of cathedral, rising
in velvety grey-black stone from two-storey red brick houses, he
said. The stone has been restored to its original, lighter colour but
an impression of darkness amid satanic mills remains. I was there
for choral evensong, St Peter-at-Leeds being one of two parish
churches in the country with daily choral services; the other is
Tewkesbury Abbey.

To enter this church from the descending darkness of an evening
in Leeds is an almost overwhelming sensual and spiritual experience. A powerful scent of white lilies, left over from a wedding
the day before, rose up behind the assembled church wardens,
dressed as if for dinner in a grey silk tie, grey trousers, black tailcoat
and waistcoat, greeting and handing the 1662 Book of Common
Prayer to the two dozen worshippers, largely middle-aged and
older, arriving in ones and twos. 'Leeds parish church has a
spaciousness and grandeur which grows on you after the first
gasp of amazement,' Betjeman said. The combination of dark
carvings, red carpets, stained glass, an imposing gallery and a
massive carved organ was almost shocking in its extravagance.

The service, a superb performance of high church ritual in strict accordance with Protestant tradition, began with a procession, a crucifer leading the choir of men in red and white cassocks and surplices. As we began the first hymn the clergy, in black cassocks and white surplices, came in, the rector, the Rev. Stephen Oliver, and the curate, both wearing choir habit with scarf and hood.

The congregation, scattered throughout the galleried nave, should have appeared insignificantly small amid such grandeur. But none seemed awed, and we knelt and stood in comfortable unison. One of the church's eight wardens read from the Old Testament. 'And behold the Lord passed by, and a great and strong wind rent the mountains,' he said, his words complemented by a sound of rushing wind as the organ, which occupies the entire south transept, warmed up for its thunderous rendition of the 'Magnificat'.

Outside, beyond the dark wood rafters, freezing cold rain scattered over the eaves and stern tracery. Inside, the warm darkness of the church, its dark-stained polished oak which turned out to be painted papier-mâché and plaster gleaming in the fading light, was redolent of a Church of England which I had thought was long gone.

The 'Nunc Dimittis', the 'lesser litany', Lord's Prayer, versicles and responses were all sung by the choir of men, while the curate, the Rev. Paul Hunt, a haunting tenor, sang the collects.

The ritual continued, beautiful and moving. For the sermon, the senior verger and registrar, Douglas Longstaffe, bowed to Mr Hunt in his seat in the choir, led him in procession to the foot of the tall, elaborately carved pulpit and bowed again. Mr Hunt ascended the graceful staircase and we crossed ourselves as he began: 'In the name of the father . . .' His sermon combined the prosaic with the spiritual. He described how he had been neglecting his household chores and had decided to make amends to his wife by cleaning the lavatory. Hours later his back seized up, landing him in bed for several weeks. This had given him time to think, and he had discovered he was not indispensable. He had also discovered a sense of how it might feel to be unemployed.

'This parish, whose life I share, has continued celebrating the love of God through worship, prayer and service, even though I have been laid up,' he said. 'It has made me face up to how important to me it is to feel needed.' Afterwards the rector led the intercessions: 'O God, give us work all our lives and give us life until our work is done.' After a warm cup of coffee and gentle gossip, we returned to the dismal winds of Leeds city centre, with peace in our hearts.

SUNDAY SERVICES: Holy Communion (1662) 9.15 a.m.; sung eucharist (Rite A) 10.30 a.m.; evensong 3 p.m. in winter and 6.30 p.m. from March to November.

Mount St Bernard Abbey
Coalville
LEICESTER
LE67 5UL
(Tel: 01530 832298/832022)

ABBOT: The Rt Rev. John Moakler.

ARCHITECTURE: Severe, undecorated Gothic style by Augustus Pugin, best-known architect of Gothic revival.

SERMON: Guidance on how to discern the legitimacy of pronouncements by those in authority.

MUSIC: Digital Allen organ, with monks singing psalms, and a chant before Gospel reading.

LITURGY: From the ordinary Catholic missal, using the Revised Standard Version of the Bible for the readings.

AFTER-SERVICE CARE: Coffee and biscuits in the guesthouse, mainly for those on retreat.

SPIRITUAL HIGH: Unexpectedly uplifting in its simplicity.

Asceticism, the spiritual discipline of self-denial as practised by the forty Cistercian monks of Mount St Bernard Abbey, has been unfashionable for the past three decades. But among Roman Catholics, in the Midlands at least, the signs are that it has retained its appeal.

The Cistercians are an enclosed order, living by the rule of St Benedict. The order began at the end of the eleventh century and was given its basic structure by Stephen Harding, an Englishman, in his Charter of Charity.

At the hour-long community mass I attended, the music was technically not brilliant; the liturgy and homily were quiet, although the sound system has now been repaired, and the church was a little chilly, even though it was mid-August. I had expected that the mass, starting at 9 a.m. and celebrated several miles from the nearest big centre of population, Leicester, would be poorly attended, yet almost every seat was taken, as at the 8 a.m. mass.

More than 300 people attend mass at the abbey each week: between twenty and thirty staying at the monastic guesthouse. As the abbey has no parish of its own, the figures are impressive. Kneeling beneath the severe grey stone Gothic arches it was not difficult to see the appeal. Sister Catherine Ronan, one of two Franciscan missionary nuns on retreat at the abbey, said: 'It is extremely prayerful and restful; even just watching the monks pray. People are attracted to the atmosphere of prayer and quiet.' The word 'monk' derives from the Greek word *monos*, meaning alone. In this big but silent congregation of all ages, I felt truly alone, though not lonely.

Few people spoke to each other, at beginning or end, and the singing was muted. So I used this opportunity for contemplation to imagine I was in one of the many Cistercian abbeys dissolved by Henry VIII. The ruins of these can still be seen around the countryside. The architect, Augustus Pugin (1812–52), borrowed from these remains, and it was inspiring to experience the form these communities might have taken.

The principal celebrant for our mass was Father Thomas Le Blanc Smith, aged eighty, who converted from Anglicanism sixty years ago. As a loud bell sounded the hour, the organ began playing and a procession of monks filed into the sanctuary between the transepts and beneath the bell tower. Some of the monks of the abbey are ordained priests; others, known as brothers, are not.

The twenty priests were vested in green chasubles as at an ordinary mass; the fifteen brothers wore habits of white cowl and black scapular. Although the average age of the community (sixty-two years) is increasing, it is attracting youngsters: two postulants, who were admitted as novices, wore jeans and jumpers.

The mass began with the monks seated in a circle in the sanctuary. They joined in the psalm for the morning office of terce in antiphonal English plainchant, led by Father Peter, the cantor, who has a striking tenor voice. Some of the congregation joined in the responses; most were content to listen.

Throughout the service, four candles burnt on the altar, and the mass was dominated by an imposing, large, wooden crucifix suspended by chains from one of the arches over the sanctuary. The reserved sacrament was in a 'hanging pyx', a form of tabernacle suspended from the bell tower, with the sanctuary lamp above.

In his homily, which followed readings from the Old and New Testaments and the Gospel of St Matthew, Fr Thomas addressed the question of authority.

'All legitimate authority comes from God,' he said. 'That is when we are bound to obey so long as that authority is legitimate. Always, if we see this authority acting legitimately, we should obey, because we are in fact obeying God, obeying Christ.' But, he added: 'We are at liberty to disobey when that authority goes beyond its own limits.' An individual should obey 'in order to do God's will and not simply to curry favour'. Authority must be seen as 'a form of service' and not a means of domineering.

After a short silence, we moved into the Creed. When the bread and wine had been taken to the altar at the offertory, a censer (thurible) was swung over them, dispersing incense. The most unusual part was the joining together of the many voices of the priests in reciting the eucharistic prayer.

The mass seemed brief and to the point, but it seemed to give everybody what they needed: a time to rest and pray before the week ahead.

SUNDAY SERVICES: Mass 8 a.m.; community mass 9 a.m. with the monks; vespers 5.15 p.m.

Liverpool Christian Life Centre,
1–11 Cornwallis Street,
LIVERPOOL
(Tel: 0151–709 0749)

SENIOR MINISTER: John Partington.

ARCHITECTURE: An impression of surreality. The Victorian warehouse, formerly a workshop for blind people, is in a notorious red light area and surrounded by houses with barred windows.

SERMON: Rousing, with experience of evangelism mixed with a Bible college-trained delivery.

MUSIC: Electric guitars, drums and a synthesiser led us in a series of Christian pop songs, with unusual improvisation when one female vocalist was inspired 'by the spirit of the Lord'.

LITURGY: Communion was accompanied by relevant Bible verses.

AFTER-SERVICE CARE: Tea, coffee and biscuits in cafe-like area.

SPIRITUAL HIGH: Difficult, even for a sceptic, to resist the excitement and enthusiasm that come from real change taking place in people's lives.

The often-told story of church decline in Britain is difficult to reconcile with that of the Assemblies of God, the UK's biggest pentecostal grouping, with more than 600 churches and nearly 50,000 members. In the five years to 1990, church membership grew by 20 per cent. The Liverpool Christian Life Centre, founded in 1989 with twelve people in the home of its minister, John Partington, is one of the fastest growing. Congregations in a warehouse now number 400 or more, and the centre has 'planted', or founded, a further eight congregations, who will eventually become part of the Assemblies of God, a fellowship of autonomous churches.

In a charismatic pentecostal church, worship reflects a belief that the gifts received by the first Christians on the day of Pentecost, recorded in Acts and Corinthians, can be exercised today. They include prophecy, healing, exorcism and speaking in tongues, and usually come after the convert has been 'baptised in the Holy Spirit'.

On my visit, the centre reflected the pentecostal tradition's roots as a church for the poor. Members were well dressed and smiling. Their eyes shone, and they seemed almost to glow with faith. Their enthusiasm was difficult to resist. But many were from the city's most deprived areas. Nearly all I met said they had, through their conversion, recovered from lives of desperation, including for some sleeping rough, dealing in drugs and being on the run from police.

The church was celebrating an auction which, with the help of a signed Liverpool football, had raised £1,300 for a staircase. New windows gleamed throughout, thanks to a convert who is a glazier. Pot plants brightened the drab interior. There was a creche, a shop selling baby equipment, a youth room and a shower room. The basement is to be converted into a gym and sauna.

'The commission of the Gospels is to help the poor,' Mr Partington said. 'I really do believe that the Gospel is practical and social, as well as spiritual. Working in this area, you have to believe that.' As the service began, members patrolled the streets with walkie-talkies to safeguard our cars from theft. We opened with a gospel song, as people danced and dozens of hands went into the air.

Mr Partington is a charismatic leader. Walking back and forths across the stage, with a microphone, he worked the congregation up to fever pitch. He asked how many had come to sing praises to their God, and was answered by cheers.

We celebrated communion, called here the 'taking of the emblems'. Sometimes wine is used but this week it was grape juice, served in small glasses, and leavened bread.

Our prayers were illustrated. A detailed map of the trouble spots in the former Yugoslavia was projected on to the screen. We were told to choose one area and pray for it.

A young man, Alan Vance, preached in a strong Nottingham accent that belied his American tele-evangelist looks. He described visiting an old haunt, a pub, with his brother after his conversion: 'The same lads were playing pool, a bit fatter and a bit uglier. The juke box was playing "One Day at a Time, Sweet Jesus". I went to the barman and said, "Can I talk to these fellows about Jesus?" Everyone went quiet. I unplugged the juke box. My brother backed away, white-faced. I said: "All those that want some prayer, follow me to the toilet." Forty people followed me. I cannot say every one of those went to God, but people remember.

'I was on so much of a high. I went to the next pub, took the mike at the disco, and about five people came to the toilet this time.' He was seventeen at the time, and precocious. He recounted another story. 'As soon as I got saved, I took tracts down to where the bikers and prostitutes were. My knees were shaking. I threw the whole lot in the door and ran off.

'I didn't look behind me but it made an impact. If nothing else, it made an impact on me.' Inspired, fifty people went to the front of the church. Mr Partington took over to lead trained counsellors in a laying-on of hands. 'In the name of Jesus, receive that which comes through these hands,' he said. 'Receive his healing.' We sang a little more before the benediction and a final amen.

Afterwards, a queue of people waited to tell me their story. Tony Wilson, aged twenty-six, said he had dealt in and used drugs, spent time in prison, studied the occult and lost everything before going to church: 'They had their hands in the air. My head was saying get out. But something in my heart changed and I asked Jesus into my life.' Pentecostals are accustomed to mockery for their apparently simplistic beliefs. While none can guarantee that their hopes for the next life will be fulfilled, few doubt that life with the Assembly of God is better than life without it.

SERVICES: Sunday pre-service prayer 9.45 a.m.;, All Together Celebration 10.30 a.m.; Kids' Explosion 10.30 a.m.; Tues: ACTS Bible school 7.30 p.m.; Weds and Thurs: Home Groups Fellowships; Fri: Youth Alive (11–16s) Club 16–30 (17–30s) (Tel: 0151–709 7977/7120).

The Church of the Immaculate Conception
Farm Street
LONDON W1
(Tel: 0171–493 7811)

PARISH PRIEST: Fr Michael Beattie SJ.

ARCHITECTURE: Decorated Gothic, lofty.

SERMON: Brief and to the point, intellectually challenging but also accessible. Jesuit theologians sometimes preach.

MUSIC: Out of this world.

LITURGY: Solemn Latin mass surprisingly easy to follow, with musical notation and English translation.

AFTER-SERVICE CARE: Excellent coffee and tea. Priest busy preparing for next mass, but worshippers happy to chat.

SPIRITUAL HIGH: Flawless and impeccable.

Farm Street, the Jesuit church in the heart of Mayfair, London, has gained an unfair reputation of exclusivity, thanks partly to its privileged site, and its association with the rich and famous, and with novelists such as Evelyn Waugh. Less is made of the social action of the parish and the Jesuit fathers. The church has its own branch of the Society of St Vincent de Paul, parishioners who help the poor, and is linked with the Daughters of Charity in nearby Blandford Street, who work with the sick and deprived.

For an Anglican, unable to take communion in a Roman Catholic church and thus offered a blessing instead, the priests at Farm Street (officially known as the Church of the Immaculate Conception) give one of the most spiritual blessings in London. Even today the Jesuits have a reputation as a somewhat sinister society, a hangover from 1580, when the Jesuit mission came to England from Rome and was seen as part of a Papist plot to overthrow Elizabeth I. Subsequently, Jesuits were thought by many to be the prime culprits in the Gunpowder Plot of 1605, although they had in fact worked hard to discourage the conspiracy.

After the Catholic Emancipation of 1829, when restrictions on belief and worship were removed from Roman Catholics, Jesuits were allowed to stay, but they were not allowed to recruit novices and were thus expected to die out. Fortunately for the homeless and deprived, not only did the Jesuits ignore these restrictions and survive, but they went from strength to strength.

Of the eight available Sunday masses at Farm Street, about 500 Roman Catholics, a few Anglicans and I chose to attend the only Latin mass, at 11 a.m. Fortunately for all adult survivors of a modern education, congregants are issued with a booklet with an English translation alongside the Latin. This was not the old Tridentine mass, which can be celebrated with the special permission of the diocesan bishop only, but the new order of mass in line with the decrees of the Second Vatican Council (1962–65). Many young Catholics from the Continent were present, and some said they preferred the Latin mass. 'Whichever country we are in, we feel at home because we are all speaking the same language,' one French student said.

Apart from the Paternoster and the occasional Deo gratias we took little active part, but instead sat back, stood up or knelt down to enjoy the world-renowned Farm Street Singers' spectacular rendition of Mozart's *Spaurmesse*. As is universal in the Catholic church, readings were in the vernacular. The Second Reading and bidding prayers were delivered by women. More than half the thirty official readers for the 11 o'clock solemn mass at Farm Street are women.

At the lively coffee morning which followed the service I was welcomed enthusiastically by a succession of voluble Irish, French and English men and women. Many Anglican churches with seating for 900 people seem over-large, but Farm Street seems barely big enough, with more than 1,400 people of all ages at mass each Sunday, plus 250 at daily mass. The order, founded in Rome by St Ignatius of Loyola, was established by Pope Paul III in 1540. The church, the work of the architect J.J. Scoles, dates from the 1840s, and was built in the stables and coachmen's quarters in a street which took its name from the eighteenth-century Hay Hill Farm.

There seemed to be a marked absence of children and babies, until the parish priest, Fr Michael Beattie SJ, pointed out that they were all in the 'crying room', the chapel of St Ignatius, to the left of the high altar. The chapel has been sealed with soundproof glass. A loudspeaker pipes in the music and liturgy for the parents, but only the nearest congregants hear the occasional muted cry. St Ignatius, with his concern for the education of the young, would surely approve. The church also has a super-efficient 'deaf loop'. This means the hard of hearing not only hear the service but the occasional *sotto voce* comments in the sanctuary which Fr Beattie lets slip giving new meaning to Christ's ability to make the deaf hear.

Unusually, this was the feast day for two saints. It was the last Sunday of the Catholic liturgical year and thus the feast of Christ the King; and the calendar date was the feast day of St Cecilia, patroness of music.

Anglicans who are considering going over to Rome should take into account the fact that many Catholic churches have two collections. Farm Street worshippers give a total of £1,400 a week. The first collection, usually the bigger, goes to the upkeep of the church and the second to diocesan work, social needs and education. To the delight of music lovers, Fr Beattie announced that the second collection, taken at the Latin mass, would from now on support the choir, all professional musicians. A professional recording has been made of the choir, led by Nicholas Danby, the internationally renowned organist.

MASS TIMES: Saturday 6 p.m.; Sunday 7.30 a.m., 8.30 a.m., 10 a.m., 11 a.m. (Latin), 12.15 p.m., 4.15 p.m., 6.15 p.m.; daily 7.30 a.m., 8.30 a.m., 12.05 a.m., 1 p.m., 6 p.m.; Saturday: 7.30 a.m., 8.30 a.m., 11 a.m. A confessor is always available at the church house at 114 Mount Street, London W1.

Hinde Street Methodist Church
The West London London Mission
Corner of Hinde Street and Thayer Street
LONDON W1M 5LJ
(Tel: 0171–935 6179)

SUPERINTENDENT MINISTER: The Rev. David Cruise.

ARCHITECTURE: Classical with a two-storey portico and small dome reminiscent of St Paul's cathedral. Built in 1887 for £16,500 along the lines of a traditional Methodist preaching chapel, and recently refurbished.

SERMON: Powerful and compelling preaching by Lord Soper, aged ninety, who can also be heard at Speaker's Corner in Hyde Park each Sunday.

MUSIC: Some inspired singing from the choir.

LITURGY: Strongly traditional, strictly Methodist, but with the appearance of being more Anglican than many Anglican churches today.

AFTER-SERVICE CARE: Coffee after each service, and a church lunch on the first Sunday of the month.

SPIRITUAL HIGH: Low church at its highest.

Lord Soper's worldwide reputation as a soap-box preacher has diverted attention from his other talents. His dignified and impressive style can be enjoyed elsewhere than in the freezing wind at Tower Hill or Hyde Park, where hecklers compete with his Gospel message each Wednesday and Sunday for the interest of the listener.

At 10 a.m. on Sunday, Lord Soper celebrates communion at the Hinde Street Methodist Church, at the corner of Hinde Street and Thayer Street in the West End. His great age would lead me to advise an early visit, except that Lord Soper gives the impression of energy enough to last a century more. We were there on his ninetieth birthday, but the only sign of his age was a certain discomfort as he climbed the step to the communion table. He appeared little older than most members of his congregation.

Even in midwinter, the Hinde Street church exudes an atmosphere redolent of summer seaside worship. The semicircular galleried interior, painted in pale blue and cream, with light

brown carpets and blue vinyl-padded chairs, and with sunlight
filtering through stained-glass windows, was redolent of a seaside
end-of-pier theatre. However, a recent facelift both inside and out
has brought out the original, dignified beauty of this historic place
of worship.

The small wooden table with a lace altar cloth was overshadowed
by the most enormous pulpit behind it, an indication of the
Methodist church's emphasis on preaching. Because it was Lord
Soper's birthday, the church was full to overflowing, but the usual
turnout for the morning communion is about twenty.

About 150 people turn up for the 11 a.m. service and about
eighty, mainly students in their twenties and thirties, for the more
informal evening service. On entering, it is not unusual to pass a
sad panoply of drunk and homeless men, some of whom sleep on
the church steps in cardboard boxes, although on this Sunday they
had found another haven. The presence of such people reflects
the fact that this church also provides the worshipping heart of
the outreach work of the West London Mission, which runs two
day centres for homeless people, residential rehabilitation for those
who abuse alcohol, and a probation hostel. It seeks to serve some
of the most needy people in the community, and has the strapline:
'Good news for those who need it most'.

Lord Soper wore a black cassock and green preacher's scarf.
We were using the 1936 liturgy, a rite with close similarities to
the Anglican Book of Common Prayer. We acknowledged and
bewailed our manifold sins and wickedness, as do traditionalist
Anglicans. Lord Soper occasionally departed from the liturgy, but
always with an immaculate style born of experience.

'All who so desire are welcome to our Lord's table,' he began,
later inserting the occasional 'we beseech thee' where none had
existed previously.

For communion we received white bread broken into squares
instead of wafers, and grape juice instead of wine. Lord Soper
would normally preach at communion, but on this occasion the
sermon had been transferred to morning worship at 11 a.m., so
I stayed on to listen. It was worth the wait, and the music at
the second service, with the choir singing from the gallery, was
outstanding.

'What a world we live in,' said Lord Soper. 'Children no longer
obey their parents and everybody wants to write a book.' He
referred to the Bourbons, the former French royal family. 'It is
recorded that they forgot nothing but learnt nothing,' he said.

He also mentioned his own longevity. 'I have now come to know that if I get through the Methodist conference, I always live to the end of the year.' The conference is the governing body of the Methodist church, which meets each summer and has a reputation for testing the stamina of the youngest man.

Lord Soper's main thrust was the debate over doubt and faith, truth and falsehood, which has occupied the churches for most of his lifetime. He based his sermon on the three Christian graces of faith, hope and charity, which, amid all the doubts surrounding the literal truth of the Resurrection and the Virgin Birth, have stood the test of time. 'The Christian Church today has to embark as never before on a fellowship of controversy, that out of that controversy there may come an acclamation of truth, an increase in belief,' he said.

He spoke for a long time, maybe half an hour, longer than most preachers today could get away with. But the congregation hung on every word. 'I have found in my ministry that the practice of good works is the generation of love,' he said. 'I do not think we would have engaged at the West London Mission in caring for alcoholics if we had tested the problem in terms of how much we like the job.'

SUNDAY SERVICES: Holy Communion 10 a.m.; morning worship with crèche, junior and youth fellowship 11 a.m.; evening worship along more informal and meditative lines, with communion on the second and fourth Sundays of the month 6.30 p.m.

All Souls Langham Place
2 All Souls Place
LONDON
W1N 3DB
(Tel: 0171–580 3522)

RECTOR: Prebendary Richard Bewes.
ARCHITECTURE: Gothic and classical, vivid impression of gold and light.
SERMON: Amusing but spiritual.
MUSIC: Popular classical with old and modern, good if you like singing.
LITURGY: Basic.
AFTER-SERVICE CARE: Tea, coffee, cold drinks and biscuits. Sunday lunches and suppers plus a newcomers' desk.
SPIRITUAL HIGH: Where lost souls find themselves and God.

At Christmas, towards the end of their annual carol service each year, hundreds of young Christians, led by a band of musicians, troop out of All Souls church to serenade patients at the Middlesex Hospital in nearby Mortimer Street. Anyone who enjoys a midwinter sing-along should be there.

All Souls, opposite Broadcasting House in Portland Place, has been used regularly by the BBC for the daily service and has a reputation as the evangelical church of the establishment. As many as 2,000 people, 75 per cent of them younger than thirty-five, attend the three services each Sunday, and the carol service has become so popular that it has been divided into three, beginning at the start of Advent.

This is one large church where there is no need to wrap up warmly in mid-winter. The large number of bodies packed close together quickly raises the temperature to a sleep-inducing heat, but it was fortunate that we had the Rev. Simon Parke, then the curate but who has since moved on, as our preacher. He not only kept the congregation wide awake after an hour of non-stop carols, but reduced us to laughter by taking as the text for his sermon a British Rail announcement.

In comparing waiting for Christmas to waiting for a British Rail train, he was fervent and fiery, gesticulating often, but ending on a suitably sombre note. 'What is happening to England, let alone the rest of the world? The most famous excuse for late trains is the wrong type of snow. But what we are looking at here as we wait for Christmas is the wrong type of world.'

In many ways, the ministry team of nine, headed by the rector, the Rev. Richard Bewes, avoids overt identification with the Church of England. This is in order not to alienate the large numbers of foreigners and non-believers, or 'seekers after truth', who show up each week.

All Souls is renowned for its music. The full sixty-strong All Souls orchestra, founded by the director of music, Noel Tredinnick, in 1972, can be heard at the church on the third Sunday in the month, and most other services are led by a band of about eleven.

Central London can hardly be envisaged without this church, although John Nash's design was lampooned extensively after the building was completed in 1823. One MP raised the subject in the House of Commons in 1824, asking who was responsible for 'such a monstrosity'. A cartoonist depicted Nash impaled on the spire.

Today the pews have gone, replaced by cushioned chairs, and All Souls is fitted out with the latest in sound and video technology. 'No ear may hear his coming,' we sang, from 'O Little Town of Bethlehem', and it was startling at this point to see a white projector screen descend from the ceiling to obscure an enormous painting depicting Christ in the hands of his enemies. The lights dimmed, and Mr Bewes led us in the closing prayers, accompanied by slide projections of Christmas in Bethlehem. In such an atmosphere, the hopes and fears of the past year seemed bearable at last.

SUNDAY SERVICES: Holy Communion, 9.30 a.m.; main services, 11 a.m. and 6.30 p.m.; mid-week lunchtime service Thursday, 1.05–1.35 p.m. Plus midweek training in Christian ministry, student groups, Sunday School and creche, fellowship groups and groups for new Christians.

The Salvation Army
Regent Hall
275 Oxford Street
LONDON W1R 1LD
(Tel: 0171–629 5424)

OFFICER-IN-CHARGE: Major David Drake.

ARCHITECTURE: Late nineteenth century, known as 'The Rink' because it was converted from a roller-skating rink.

ADDRESS: Distillation of spiritual need 'which can only be fully met in Jesus Christ':

MUSIC: Fabulously rousing renditions from a sixty-strong 'Songster Brigade' and a 'Singing Company' of twenty, accompanied at times by a surprisingly youthful and expert brass band.

LITURGY: No set order, but meetings structured around music and song.

AFTER-SERVICE CARE: Great if you are an alcoholic. down-and-out, homeless, lost, unemployed, spiritually bereft or simply seeking friendship.

SPIRITUAL HIGH: Elevating to the point where I almost wanted to sign up.

Transfixed by glistening goods in windows and counting off the shopping days to Christmas, I almost missed the small, drab doorway squeezed between Ernest Jones and Scottish Woollens, opposite BhS in Oxford Street, London.

But behind it lurked a remarkable interior. Purchased by the Salvation Army in 1882, the former roller-skating rink is now a worship centre of military splendour, with polished wood and banners at ease beside the Bibles and songbooks, and a crest like a target on the wall bearing the motto 'Blood and Fire', the blood of Christ and the fire of the Holy Spirit.

A few veterans and Salvation Army stalwarts, wearing the distinctive navy blue uniforms, had turned out for the 9.30 a.m. prayers which began the Sunday programme. By 10 a.m. the brass band, including young solicitors, doctors, accountants, computer operators, barristers and retired businessmen, was gathered in the lobby and ready to march, with Sergeant Major Colin Ambrose at the head. A woman percussionist struck up on the drums, and as the band marched out into Oxford Street we fell in behind.

It was impossible not to walk in time to the music, or to escape a thrill as the Number Seven bus was forced to a halt, foreign tourists stared, and even builders on the roadside were reduced to slack-jawed silence. A guiding principle of the Salvation Army is that if the people won't come to church, they will take the church to them.

The Salvation Army, founded by William Booth, the Methodist preacher, in 1865, has territories in ninety-five countries worldwide, with 1.5 million soldiers and 16,455 officers. A further four territories have been established in the former Soviet Union, but without proper constitutions. The Salvation Army is run along military lines. Worldwide, it is divided into territories, provinces and divisions, with a general at its head and ranks of commissioners, colonels, lieutenant-colonels, majors, captains and lieutenants below. Each officer is an ordained minister of religion. The Salvation Army has corps, not churches, which are army units established for the propagation of the Gospel. Soldiers are non-commissioned corps members who attend Sunday meetings and have signed a declaration of Christian faith, where they promise to lead a life of high moral value and to abstain from smoking, drinking and gambling.

Harris Gianaros, aged thirty-two, the hall manager, had joined the army a month before, 'because they put Christianity into practice'. He marched behind with us. By now we had reached Lilley & Skinner, turned left past Bond Street station and right again, stopping opposite a Victorian red-brick block of flats, behind whose tightly drawn curtains unsuspecting residents were sleeping.

Bandsman Gavin Drake, a business studies student, who plays the euphonium, led our worship, reading out every verse of every hymn so those without books could sing along. We launched enthusiastically into 'Life is Great! So Sing About It!' A middle-aged woman in a nightgown appeared at the door of the flats. She was about to speak her mind but changed it at the last minute, and accepted instead a copy of *The War Cry*, the Salvation Army newspaper which sells 85,000 copies a week. The number of onlookers had crept up to six when we reached the prayers.

'Dear Lord, we pray for each and every person in this street,' said bandsman Ken Bonser-Ward. A dustcart drove up the street and down again, stalling for just a little too long beside us for it to be chance. 'Have you ever stopped to think how God loves you?'

we sang joyfully to the driver, whose cynical expression melted in the face of this religious advance, and who surrendered and drove away. After a brief talk from a bandsman, urging listeners to read their Bibles, we sang a final song and turned about. The builders this time cheered us back into the hall.

This was just the beginning to the Salvation Army Sunday, a 'day of rest' which went on to include more open-air meetings, songs and worship in the hall. This intensive programme gave little clue to the vast amount of social work and caring that goes on behind the scenes. In London alone, the Salvation Army runs hostels for homeless people and alcoholics, organises soup runs for the homeless, helps abused children, traces missing people, runs play-centres, nurseries and employment training centres. Regent Hall is one of 900 worship centres in the UK, attended by more than 55,000 soldiers as well as the public.

Salvation Army officers tend to work in couples. If an officer wishes to marry, he or she must marry another officer, a rule which allows 'swift movement of troops when given their marching orders', according to one member. Captain John Wainwright and Mrs Captain Dorita Wainwright led the next act of worship, for which the Rink was packed with Salvation Army members, tourists, local residents and young families, and the numbers grew as the day progressed. But my lasting impression was the excitement at the unlikely meeting of God and Mammon, when we marched out into Oxford Street, not to shop, but to sing and pray.

SUNDAY WORSHIP: at Regent Hall: prayer meeting 9.30 a.m.; open-air meeting or hospital visit 10 a.m.; morning worship 11 a.m.; lunch 12 noon; open-air meeting 1.45 p.m.; musical praise and tea 2.45 p.m.; open-air meeting 5.30 p.m.; Good News for Today 6 p.m.

The Queen's Chapel of the Savoy
Savoy Street
LONDON
WC2
(Tel: 0171–836 7221)

CHAPLAIN: The Rev. John Robson, Chaplain of the Royal Victorian Order.
ARCHITECTURE: Slightly bleak but evocative.
SERMON: Moving, modest, with personal appeal.
MUSIC: Heavenly.
LITURGY: Traditional Book of Common Prayer.
AFTER-SERVICE CARE: Handshake, longer than usual chat with clergy, sherry in the Queen's robing room first Sunday of the month.
SPIRITUAL HIGH: Dignified.

People whose faith in the Church of England as part of the one holy, catholic and apostolic Church was shaken by the General Synod vote in support of women priests could do no better than take a restorative dose of worship at the Queen's Chapel of the Savoy. There the Rev. John Robson, the chaplain, is honest enough to admit he once opposed women priests because he believed the church to be essentially paternalistic. He has come round. 'Under God it has happened and under God we must try to make it work,' he said, somewhat sadly, at the end of his sermon.

Hitherto unsuspected and enigmatic overtones seemed attached to the church's decision in this chapel, a Chapel of Her Majesty the Queen in right of her Duchy of Lancaster. In the rousing rendition of the national anthem which opened the service we sang: 'Long live our noble Duke', as a reminder that the Queen is also Supreme Governor of the Church of England.

The chapel is sought out regularly by wealthy Americans and other tourists staying in the many hotels on the Strand. It is something of an ascetic shock after the opulence of the nearest, the Savoy. But the warm intimacy of the chapel and the welcoming smiles of the regulars counteract any intimidation by the architecture. On a chilly autumnal Sunday, the oil-fired central heating felt barely adequate, but I was assured by the chaplain that it was up to the luxury standards of the Savoy Hotel.

The chapel is an oasis of traditional church music in today's ecclesiastical cultural desert of the tambourine. The choir of fourteen boys and six men is led by Dr William Cole, the master of music, who has been at the Savoy since 1954, making him one of the Church of England's longest serving men in his field. Like the chapel, Dr Cole seems to have imbibed some miraculous preservative, and appears little changed by the passage of time.

The worshippers on my visit were also timeless. Few wore hats, but the thirty or so who were there, mostly middle-aged or older, had donned their Sunday best and travelled in from as far afield as Oxford, Putney and Wimbledon to drink from the regenerative spring of tradition. All were friendly and charming, welcoming the sight of a new face.

A member of the royal family might occasionally drop by informally for worship when in London at the weekend. Like so many attractive churches, it is in great demand by couples wishing to tie the knot. For historic reasons, many are disappointed. The chapel started life as one of three which served an almshouse for 'pouer, nedie people'. Built in 1512 by Henry VII, it was taken over by the Duchy of Lancaster in 1772, and in 1937 became the chapel of the Royal Victorian Order by command of King George VI. As such it is now a 'free' chapel, without a parish and not falling under any ecclesiastical jurisdiction. Couples need a special archbishop's licence to marry there. Couples who do succeed in meeting the stringent requirements and acquiring one of the sought-after licences get a special reward: they meet for a romantic re-run of their weddings at a special Valentine service each February, when they renew their vows. Thus are many enticed to stay within the worshipping fold.

Historic names associated with the chapel include the fourteenth-century churchman Wycliffe, plus Chaucer, Samuel Pepys and John of Gaunt. It lies in the heart of the five-acre Savoy Precinct, which hosted the 1661 Prayer Book Conference, an unsuccessful attempt to reconcile dissenters and low churchmen to the doctrine and liturgy of the Book of Common Prayer.

Unusually, the chapel runs north and south instead of east and west. The side and north walls are original, but most of the rest dates from 1864, when it was rebuilt after a fire. The roof, on the insistence of Queen Victoria, was a replica of the timber roof which perished in the fire, although it has been overpainted since. An ante-chapel and the robing room for the Queen were added in

1958. New oak panelling was also installed when the chapel was put at the disposal of the Victorian Order, but sadly the pulpit mysteriously disappeared about the same time. A candelabra containing an hour glass to help preachers judge their sermon length was on the pulpit but is now attached to the wall.

The liturgy is strictly 1662 Prayer Book. Thus we acknowledged and bewailed our manifold sins and wickedness which we, from time to time, most grievously had committed. This was a refreshing change from the more mundane, but more common, Alternative Service Book confession of sin against God and 'our fellow men'. 'The remembrance of them is grievous unto us; the burden of them is intolerable,' we said. The congregation may have had the civilised and restrained appearance associated with mainstream Anglicans, but these words were said in as heartfelt a manner as any of the more exotic confessions of personal salvation by the charismatics.

The prayer, hope and belief at the Savoy were that the church should remain united. That this tiny chapel, an island of Anglican spirituality in the midst of central London commerce, remains so strong must surely be a sign that the Church of England, too, can survive its regular upheavals with its traditional strength and dignity.

SUNDAY SERVICE: Sung communion is at 11 a.m. on the first and third Sunday of every month and on special festivals; sung matins is held on the second and fourth Sundays every month followed by a short said communion. Members of the public are welcome.

St Martin-in-the-Fields walk in aid of homeless people
Social Care Unit
6 St Martin's Place
LONDON WC2N 4JJ

VICAR: Canon Geoffrey Brown.

CARE UNIT DIRECTOR: Roger Shaljean.

ARCHITECTURE: Ancient route along bridle paths and foot-paths along the Pilgrim's Way through the chalk heartlands of Kent.

SERMON: A Carmelite friar. Fr Wilfred McGreal, addressed us briefly at an overnight stop at Aylesford priory on 'that flow of energy, even in suffering'. Speaking of Christ's journey to the cross, he said: 'When you feel despised and rejected, it is the despised and rejected one who holds out his hand to us.'

MUSIC: Entertained en route by Giles Andrews, baritone in the Philharmonia and the New Collegium Musicum, with 'Mud, Mud Glorious Mud' and songs from the musical *Salad Days*.

LITURGY: Night-time poetry reading in the graveyard at Charing.

AFTER-SERVICE CARE: Nurses massaged our feet and tenderly restored our blisters at hourly checkpoints. Sustaining food and drink in church halls and pilgrim houses along the way.

SPIRITUAL HIGH: Contemplative, ascetic and healing.

Progressing with seventy Christians along the Pilgrim's Way in Kent to raise money for homeless people, our small group lost its way after ten minutes. With a combination of faith, hope, obstinacy, and pliancy, assisted by mobile telephone, we rediscovered the path and our friends, walking the next forty miles without mishap.

The pilgrims, from the London church of St Martin-in-the-Fields, included more than twenty walkers who were or had recently been homeless, a group of helpers and a sprinkling of others whose sponsorship promised a boost to funds. Hard on the heels of John Major's description of beggars as an offensive eyesore, it provided these professionals with a valuable opportunity to listen to the stories of the homeless at first hand.

The pilgrims were sent off from Trafalgar Square with a rousing chorus of John Bunyan's 'He Who Would Valiant Be' from the Metropolitan police band. I joined the pilgrims at Swanley, and left them at Charing, before they went on to Canterbury, a total of seventy-three miles of walking.

Giles Andrews, one of the organisers, explained: 'There are laggardly Christians, speedy Christians and Christians who don't know where they are going.' Despite our rucksacks and professional-looking boots, the walk was more than a ramble, he said. 'It is for the homeless, and they walk with us.' After a couple of hours in the depths of rural Kent, civilisation seemed so far away that it was faintly alarming when, breathlessly surmounting one barley-covered hilltop, we looked back to see a star flashing on top of a distant building: it was that vast skyscraper Canary Wharf.

A night at Aylesford, a Carmelite priory founded in 1242 where we were cared for by the mendicant Whitefriars, restored our spiritual balance. We shared bread and wine at an *agape*, or 'love feast,' a brief ecumenical service where our young travelling priest, the Rev. Michael Oates, blessed the huge chunks of bread while we heard readings which spoke of freedom from the idea that 'suffering and pain were punishments for our evil ways'. Rubbing blisters and resting my aching feet, this was a message I needed to hear.

The walkers slept on concrete floors in church halls, but some of the homeless, used to 'skippering', spent the nights under the stars where they were joined by some with homes to go back to. My own sleeping bag went missing during the walk and for a few hours I felt oddly dislocated to be bagless, if not exactly homeless.

All the participants were sponsored. The previous year, the walk raised more than £10,000 for homeless people. The walk is organised annually by St Martin's Social Care Unit, which provides a drop-in advice and resettlement centre for homeless people in London. Funds from this walk will go towards a half-way house providing residential accommodation.

The busy and varied life at St Martin's has a breadth to it not wholly reflected here, because of this article's necessary concentration on the church's work with the homeless. While walking, we listened intently to the stories of walkers such as Michael, aged forty-five, who had lived in most of the cardboard cities in London, homeless 'because my family didn't want me'. He was helped into a hostel by St Martin's and is hoping to have his own place soon.

As we stopped for lunch at the beautiful, much-restored but originally medieval All Saints church at Hollingbourne, and for evensong at St Peter and St Paul in Charing, I thought of all those I might ask to sponsor me, and the inevitable refusal of some.

Then I recalled the conluding prayer of Chaucer's Wife of Bath, my own contribution to our poetry reading one night: 'And as for all old and ill-tempered skinflints, May heaven rain upon them pestilence', I vowed once more to labour night and day, and be a pilgrim.

To be a pilgrim, contact St Martin-in-the-Fields walk in aid of homeless people, Social Care Unit, 6 St Martin's Place, London WC2N 4JJ (0171–930 4137).

St Mark's Coptic Orthodox Church
Allen Street
Kensington High Street
LONDON
W8 6BL
(Tel: 0171–603 6701)

PRIEST: The Rev. Father Bishoy Boushra.

ARCHITECTURE: Defiantly Protestant from the outside, but a wooden icon screen and Egyptian stained-glass window to St Mark inside indicate an eastern theme.

SERMON: The visiting bishop took us on a long journey through early Church history, meandered off into modern social phenomena, and concluded, with admirable *gravitas*, that without God we are nothing.

MUSIC: Eastern chants accompanied at times by a cymbal and triangle.

LITURGY: Coptic liturgy of St Basil; a poetic and detailed distillation of early Christian doctrine.

AFTER-SERVICE CARE: Queue up for a face-to-face confession with the priest, or enjoy a chat beside the bookshop.

SPIRITUAL HIGH: Three hours of chanting and ritual amid clouds of incense seemed to elevate us almost into the heavens.

According to the red and black computer graphic at the front of the church, the date was 14 Baaba, the second month of the year by the calendar of the Coptic Orthodox Church. Beneath this, a dozen deacons, priests and a bishop, dressed in white, were engaged in a ritual that traces its roots to a scene in the home of St Mark.

A congregation of about 600 were deep in prayer, men on the left, women on the right. St Mark's in Kensington, west London, is the mother of the twelve Coptic churches in the UK, serving more than 10,000 Copts. The celebrant and preacher was Bishop Fam of the Tima diocese in Egypt, so our worship was largely in Arabic. Normally, the three-hour service of prayers, readings and communion is in a combination of English and Coptic, with a small part only in Arabic. Helpfully, readings and lessons were translated for us during the service.

The liturgy was compelling and intricate, and much was said, almost inaudibly, by the bishop before the altar in the sanctuary, which was almost hidden from us behind the wood and golden icon screen. Clouds of incense emanated from the sanctuary from early on, and later the front of the sanctuary, the Scriptures and the congregation were censed.

For vespers and matins, some parts of the Coptic liturgy are satisfyingly righteous, such as where the priest holds the cross, faces east and states: 'Yea, O Lord, Who gave us the authority to tread on serpents and scorpions and all powers of our enemies; crush them soon under our feet and disperse from us all their wicked intentions.' For communion, we concentrated on own sins and the lives of the saints. A reading from the Pauline epistles was followed by readings from the 'Catholicon', lessons from other epistles and from the Acts of the Apostles and the 'Sinaxarium', a collection of biographies of saints and martyrs considered complementary to the Acts.

We heard about St Philip, one of the apostles chosen by the disciples to be a deacon in the early Church. A psalm was followed by a Gospel reading, prayers and the sermon.

Along with the handful of British women there who had married Egyptians and converted, and the British-born children of Egyptian immigrants, I ascended a winding staircase into the gallery to hear a translation of Bishop Fam's half-hour discourse. Those women who would later take communion had covered their heads with lace or cotton scarves. Our translator, deacon Emanuel Joseph, whispered his way through the multitude of sins dealt with by the bishop, who fingered a cross throughout. 'The dilemma in Western countries is the lack of grace in the lives of their people,' the bishop said. 'The people of the world do not rely on the grace of God in their lives. They are always counting their money. Every penny is counted. They do not consider their blessings. Your money many times can be an obstacle to the grace of God in your lives.' We were left with about an hour for the consecration of the sacrament, the invocation to the Holy Spirit to descend upon and 'transubstantiate', or convert, the oblations into the body and blood of Christ, the prayers of intercession, the 'fraction', or the breaking of bread, and communion.

Coptic Orthodox babies can take communion from their baptism at forty days, but the non-Orthodox are asked not to and accept, instead, a chunk of the sweet, tasty, blessed but non-transubstantiated bread handed out by the priest.

Our service seemed almost as much a social as a religious event. Children and babies laughed and shouted at the back of the church, youngsters ran in and out throughout, and afterwards, over coffee, families and friends caught up on the week's news and gossip.

The Coptic Church remains the main Christian Church in Egypt, which is predominantly Muslim. The Coptic and Eastern Orthodox Churches agree on most doctrinal matters, apart from the nature of Christ. Egyptian Copts believe Christ acts always as the one 'hypostasis', the word of God incarnate. The other churches and the Copts have been separate since the Council of Chalcedon, AD 451, which taught that Christ was one person in two natures. The Copts date their year from 11 September, and their calendar began in AD 284, from the accession of the Roman emperor Diocletian, who persecuted the emerging Egyptian church and others in a period known as the Era of the Martyrs.

The Copts suffered intermittent persecution under Persian and Arab rule until the British occupation, which began in 1882, and have enjoyed freedom of worship ever since.

SUNDAY SERVICES: 9 a.m.–noon.

St Francis of Assisi Roman Catholic Parish Church
Pottery Lane
Notting Hill
LONDON
W11 4NQ
(Tel: 0171–727 7968)

PARISH PRIEST: Father Oliver McTernan.

ARCHITECTURE: A mix of Romanesque and Gothic styles, built in 1860 out of yellow London stock.

SERMON: Stirring and inspiring exposition on Isaiah.

MUSIC: The combination of foreign and traditional English hymns with a modern gospel song challenged our abilities to extemporise, but we rose to the occasion in style, helped by the strong lead from the choir.

LITURGY: From the Parish Mass Book.

AFTER-SERVICE CARE: Comfy chairs to sit and chat, with plenteous tea and coffee and heartwarming spiritual advice on modern living.

SPIRITUAL HIGH: Joyous and rich in spirit, though not shying away from the material poverty around.

Offering succour to those exhausted by the competitiveness of London life, the community centre of St Francis of Assisi is built on the spot in Notting Hill, west London, where the stables of London's Hippodrome race course once stood.

There was standing room only for those who did not arrive early for our 11.30 mass, and those of us who found a seat were squeezed shoulder-to-shoulder in the wooden pews.

The success of the Roman Catholic church of St Francis in offering spiritual nourishment to its parishioners is evident from the growing numbers. Since Fr Oliver McTernan arrived in 1981, Sunday attendance has leapt from about 350 to more than 1,100. The pews were designed to seat about 200. The parish was founded in 1859 by the Oblates of St Charles, an institute of secular priests disbanded in 1969. The Oblates were themselves founded by Dr Henry Edward Manning, an Anglican clergyman who converted to Catholicism and eventually became Archbishop of Westminster. The first priest at St Francis was Fr

Henry Rawes, also a former Anglican clergyman who went over to Rome.

The parish grew out of a mission founded in west London in the mid-nineteenth century by Cardinal Nicholas Wiseman, then Archbishop of Westminster, who identified a 'heaven-sent' opportunity to make the area a centre for the large number of Anglican clergy converting to Rome as a result of the Oxford Movement. But if the many Anglo-Catholic opponents of women priests in the Church of England today were to visit this parish in their search for a new spiritual home, they could end by judging themselves, as many others judge them, 'more Roman than the Romans'.

Fr McTernan uses non-sexist 'inclusive' language, avoiding the word 'men' where possible. In the Creed, 'for us men and our salvation' became 'for us and our salvation'. He said afterwards: 'I think it is important, because some women feel very strongly, and why alienate them unnecessarily?' Women delivered the readings from the Old and New Testament, and a woman led us in the psalm.

Fr McTernan regrets the Church of England's decision to ordain women priests. He said: 'I think it is a very difficult issue and one that won't go away. I would have preferred the Anglican church to wait for a decision by the universal Church.' I was at the monthly Filipino mass, a colourful celebration for London's several thousand immigrants from the Philippines. The Filipino association, which occupies one of the church buildings, organised the readings, and we sang hymns in Tagalog, their language. They are one of the largest groups among the sixty-four nationalities who attend St Francis nearly every week and who live within the geographical boundaries of the parish.

The freedom and joy which were almost tangible at St Francis gave an initial false impression of liberalism. In fact, this church could not be more Catholic in its spirituality, and I was reminded of this when Fr McTernan censed the altar, the cross and the congregation with the thurible, a brass casket containing burning incense and swung on a chain. This was a Catholic act of reverence preparing for the liturgical celebration, a way of focusing the mind on the sacred.

Fr McTernan preached in the aisle, striding around and achieving eye contact with as many of us as possible. His sermon was based on the Christian vocation, and the journey to faith. 'The purpose of life is not to be seen in terms of what we have around us. It is not a question of accumulating what we can in this world.

Christians have an indispensable role in relation to the world. We cannot be aloof. We cannot be indifferent.' Afterwards, as we took tea in the community centre, something more exotic filtered through to us, with sounds of Africa and hints of a stronger incense. The church had been taken over by London's Eritreans for their own weekly mass, the Gheez rite.

Fr McTernan removed his dog collar and chatted with his copious flock, and I would not have been surprised to see swans, geese and ducks fly in to join the hungry people eating bread and biscuits at this unsparing table of St Francis.

MASSES: Sunday 8, 10, 11.30 a.m., 6.30 p.m.; Gheez rite 1 p.m. Saturdays: noon and 6 p.m.; weekdays: call parish office.

Hampstead Unitarian Chapel, 50–52 Rosslyn Hill
Hampstead
LONDON
NW3 ISB
(Tel: 0171–435 3506)

MINISTER: Rev. Dr Judith Walker-Riggs.

ARCHITECTURE: Mid-nineteenth century Gothic-style, with 40ft-wide nave, indicating the importance nonconformists place on preaching. Kentish ragstone wallings and Bath stone doorways, tracery and copings.

SERMON: Chilling dissertation on the religious persecution and burning at the stake of the Roman Catholic heretic Giordano Bruno, whose crimes included opposing Aristotelian doctrines and supporting Copernicus.

MUSIC: Organ and hymns, and a short piano recital.

LITURGY: Secularised hymns, poems and short readings.

AFTER-SERVICE CARE: Freshly brewed coffee and date brownies, and the opportunity to debate theology with free-thinkers from Hampstead and as far afield as St Albans. Congregation goes for a pub lunch once a month.

SPIRITUAL HIGH: A rare feeling that freedom of thought, expression and conscience were acceptable and welcome.

God came into the service at the Hampstead Unitarian chapel, north London, only briefly, and then obliquely. 'Let us join together in a spirit of prayer and meditation,' said the minister.

'O thou great force of life, who some call God and others find too large to name at all, we live as part of thy blessed universe, so small upon the face of the earth, mere dots upon the infinite sea.' This was the closest we came to traditional prayer in the hour-long service in this beautiful, honey and grey-coloured chapel. Although crosses featured in some of the stained glass, and in the decor, there was no mention of Christ. We sang from an unashamedly liberal hymn book, with strange words, to familiar tunes, such as 'Morning has Broken'. In the leaflet handed to me at the door, Dr Walker-Riggs gives a flavour of what was to come. 'I am an unrepentant theist, atheist, agnostic, mystic humanist,' she says.

Unitarianism, which has about 10,000 members in Britain but is strong in America, is on the edge of the Christian tradition. As a distinct religion, it dates from the Reformation era. Unitarians reject the doctrine of the Trinity and the deification of Christ: they believe that Christ, along with all human beings, partakes of the divinity. They have no formal creed and are guided chiefly by reason and conscience. Church literature draws on the modern language of psychology.

The church encourages people 'to discover themselves', to embark on a 'search for truth' throughout their lives. Unitarians are people 'trying to make sense of life', and who have respect for the truth in themselves and in others.

To confess openly to Unitarianism remained a legal offence in Britain until 1813. Many, including the scientist Sir Isaac Newton, thought it safer to conform outwardly to the Church of England. It is a matter of pride at Hampstead that a congregation of 'protestant dissenters' began worshipping there in 1692, and had become Unitarian for many years before the lifting of the legal ban.

Our service began with the lighting of a candle in a chalice by a member of the congregation, Mary Broughton-Wilson, who said: 'Lighting the chalice is a celebration in my life, to say thank you to everybody who supported me so much last year when I was so ill.' Dr Walker-Riggs, formerly a minister in Kansas City, Missouri, continued: 'We are here to be made whole, to set aside all that fractures us or makes us frantic, and to allow ourselves to be touched by that which is as constant as breathing or heart beats. We pray to let our reason and our passion keep us true to ourselves, true to each other and true to our vision of what we can together become.' Then followed some of the most challenging church notices I have heard. We were invited to sandwich-making for the homeless, an open-air concert at nearby Kenwood, to support a Traidcraft stall selling coffee, dried fruits and spices after the service, and to donate money, food and clothes to those in need.

Few can leave the chapel without doing something for someone. The jumble sales are so renowned that they can become an unruly stampede. Alison Brooks, chair of the management committee, said the church had now taken to having 'not-jumbles'. They still collect goods, but donate them direct, and cut the hassle by phoning regulars and asking them to give the money the church would have raised by selling them. The chapel looks small and quaint from outside, but inside it seemed large and spacious. A blue carpet and a variety of chairs gave it an informal feel. The chapel's tercentenary gift to itself, a £250,000 organ paid for by a legacy, is now being built up in the gallery.

Since Dr Walker-Riggs arrived in 1992, numbers have increased by a fifth to more than 150. Many in the congregation were American. Some, such as Alessandra Borbon, were ex-Catholics. Others, like William Ellington, described themselves as 'devout atheists'. They included writers, actresses, teachers, architects and others from the professional classes.

All sang heartily and listened intently as we moved into a 'naming ceremony', the Unitarian equivalent of a christening, of a baby boy, Alexander Lach. His family moved with him to the front and, in a simple ceremony, Dr Walker-Riggs gave him a red rose, to symbolise growth, life and beauty. 'To him will come giving and taking, joy and sorrow, life,' she said. We joined hands in a dedication prayer, the family took photographs and Dr Walker-Riggs read a poem: 'The child asks why and then forgets to listen. The adult listens without knowing why.' The highlight was Dr Walker-Riggs's sermon on Giordano Bruno, the Italian philosopher and Dominican who was censured for unorthodoxy, captured by the Inquisition and burnt at the stake on the Campo dei Fiori in Rome in 1600.

She said: 'He would not stop asking questions. He asked what happened to Christ's teeth. Not his adult teeth, his milk teeth, those pearls of our Lord's innocence. They fell out. When he rose on the third day, did they rise with him? If so, how? Could any of Christ's body rot? It is easy to see how the monks could go off Bruno.

'In the end he rejected the doctrine of the Trinity, not because his faith was so small, but because it was so large. He accepted the Copernican discovery that the earth was not at the centre of the universe and never had been. Bruno felt the world was so much larger than religion let it be.

'In the months following his burning, the church fell into confusion on what to say. One cardinal denied he existed, and said if he had existed, the church did not burn him.' Dr Walker-Riggs added: 'That reminds me of my son, who says: "I didn't do it, and if I did, I didn't mean to."' As a Unitarian, Dr Walker-Riggs tries to separate 'what is worth preserving and of permanent value' in the Christian religion from what has been damaging and limiting. After listening to her speak on the unfortunate Bruno, it was difficult to deny a need to do the same.

SUNDAY SERVICES: morning service 11 a.m., evening service 6 p.m.

Trinity Methodist and United Reformed Church
Golders Green
LONDON
NW11
(Tel: 0181–458 0892)

MINISTER: Rev. Dr Leslie Griffiths.

ARCHITECTURE: Imposing red-brick church built in 1928 along the lines of old preaching chapels, but attractively modernised with the pews removed and pulpit lowered.

SERMON: After a week in which many close to this church had died, Dr Griffiths touched a chord when he said: 'We do not understand the generosity of God, his magnanimity and his big-heartedness.'

MUSIC: Enthusiastic singing led by choir from the congregation. The highlight was a closing rendition of hymns by the church's own singers, Friendly Isles, otherwise known as Tonga, in frilled raffia skirts wrapped around national dress.

LITURGY: Loosely structured, largely improvised by Dr Griffiths along the lines of the traditional Methodist morning service.

AFTER-SERVICE CARE: Coffee and tea in an adjoining room.

SPIRITUAL HIGH: Grief combined with determination to rise above death and disaster.

In the fiery, impassioned style of nonconformist preachers from his native Wales, the Rev. Dr Leslie Griffiths declaimed against evil from his Methodist church pulpit in north London. Dr Griffiths, a regular contributor to Radio 4's *Thought for the Day*, was later inducted as president of the Methodist conference, the church's equivalent of the Archbishop of Canterbury, and spiritual head of the country's 1.2 million Methodists. He remained in the post for a year, and helped revive plans for unity between the Methodist church and the Church of England.

But, like most people in his crowded church that week, he was distressed, his mind on pastoral rather than ecclesiastical affairs. Barbara Rivera, a 31-year-old member of the congregation, had been killed when her Land-Rover overturned in Uganda, where she had been doing missionary work.

Her sister Vida Mei, who survived, was in church on crutches.

Another friend of the church had died, homeless, in a skip. One member had lost her father, another her mother and yet another his nephew. Dr Griffiths said: 'I do not know that there was ever such a week as this. As I prepare to go off and do other things for a little while, I feel like the shepherd abandoning his sheep.' God's approach to the messiness of human life was not mathematical, he said.

'God looks at people who are in chaos, disaster and despair and finds a way of relativising what seems to those within the gloom to be absolute, somehow opening a window so that in a darkened room a shaft of light shines and challenges the darkness.' In an age when proselytism is out and friendly co-operation with other faiths is in, this church, in the heart of north London's Jewish community, has few families nearby of the type a normal suburban church would draw on to make up its congregation. Dr Griffiths is chairman of the local Council of Christians and Jews. This church which joined with the neighbouring United Reformed church when their congregation dwindled, has, however, been saved by the presence in the neighbourhood of large numbers of trade missions and high commissions.

The congregation turned out to be an astonishing gathering of people from twenty-three different countries, many in colourful national dress. About 70 per cent were from Ghana but there were many also from the Philippines, Nigeria, Kenya and Tonga. According to John Lennard-Jones, a retired physician whose wife Verna is chairman of the local ecumenical meeting of Churches Together in England, this 'has changed the character of the church. We regard our mission as particularly to overseas people.'

Appropriately, we opened with the Old Hundredth, 'All People that on Earth do Dwell', the dignified setting gaining solemnity through the mournful, African harmonies added by grieving members of the congregation.

Scripture readings and prayers followed, but the highlight was the sermon, nearly half an hour long but dynamic and enthralling. This was a rare treat in an age when so much preaching has become dry and academic.

I left feeling that all churches, not just the Methodists, need leaders like Dr Griffiths, and hoping his gifts would not be neglected after the year end.

SUNDAY SERVICES: 10.30 a.m. and 6.30 p.m.

The Coronarium Chapel of St Katharine
St Katharine's Dock
LONDON E1 9AT
(Tel: 0171–488 4772)

CHAPLAIN: Canon Peter Delaney.

ARCHITECTURE: Simple classical rotunda with a dome. An elegant tribute to the medieval church demolished in the last century and to the engineer Thomas Telford, who went on to build the dock.

SERMON: Improvised without notes, scattered with appropriate allusions to fishing, boating and fishers of men.

MUSIC: Recitals are sometimes held in the chapel.

LITURGY: Rite A of the Church of England's Alternative Service Book.

AFTER-SERVICE CARE: No church hall makes tea and coffee impossible, but the chaplain gives expert pastoral advice and counselling in one of the numerous dockside cafes or restaurants.

SPIRITUAL HIGH: Watery fount of prayer.

The Coronarium at St Katharine's Dock in east London, so called after a competition among dock workers to find a name, is one of the smallest chapels in London, with a circumference of only a few metres. But its reach is far greater, thanks to an audio system which broadcasts Canon Peter Delaney's every word to the farthest corner of the ancient dock. Loudspeakers mounted on lampposts and office walls ensure that few of the 4,500 shop, office and restaurant workers on the St Katharine's Dock site can remain unaware of the presence of the sacred in the midst of the secular. Once the service I was attending began, the dock was launched into the rite of the Anglican communion service. 'Almighty God, to whom all hearts be open . . .' Yachtsmen and passers-by seemed almost as surprised at the presence of this ebullient Christian rite in their midst as they would have been had Neptune risen from the waves. I welcomed the protection of Simon Latham's statue of Lazarus raised from the dead by Christ, standing as a solid witness to our presence.

The Coronarium stands on a promontory linking the north

and south dock basins, behind the Tower Hotel and the Dutch swing-bridge. It was the dream of Peter Drew, former chairman of the Taylor Woodrow group, which developed the dock. Mr Drew carved the font, with its gold-leaf bowl, out of granite from the dock wall. His aim at St Katharine's was to build a community where people could live, work and play. 'Part of living, working and playing must involve recognising the existence of God and praying,' he says.

In accordance with his vision and exposed to the elements, we prayed in the presence of two catamarans, some private yachts, a ketch, an Atlantic racing yacht, some small rowing boats, six Thames barges, three longboats and the old Nore lightship from the North Sea. On a Dutch cruiser the owner downed tools to join in the Lord's Prayer. Canon Delaney waved to diners in the Tower Hotel's carvery during the 'peace', the part of the service where we all shake hands, and they waved back. Simultaneously, in the Waterside restaurant, lunchtime drinkers lifted their glasses to toast us. The sermon was based on Jesus calling his disciples to be fishers of men. Maybe Canon Delaney's action during the peace, running outside the Coronarium to shake hands with a couple of bemused tourists walking by with packets of fish and chips, was a modern-day equivalent.

The Coronarium was built in 1977. Its Perspex crown, which hangs between two pillars on the west side of the chapel, was unveiled by the Queen on her Silver Jubilee walkabout. The chapel's cast-iron columns were rescued from the original dock, and replaced in a circle on the site of the original medieval church of the Royal Foundation of St Katharine, demolished in 1826. St Katharine of Alexandria, patron saint of maidens, died a gruesome death. She was tied to a spiked wheel, rolled down a hill until the wheel broke, and finally beheaded. The instruments of her agony are alluded to in the chapel's construction: its circular shape, with pillars casting shadows like spokes across the centre.

My overall impression was of something fantastical, and this was enhanced after the service, when Canon Delaney and Terry Barber, parish clerk of nearby All Hallows by the Tower, strolled in their elaborate and ornate robes into the dockside Ivory House. This former warehouse is now converted into apartments and offices. In a sumptuous suite of modern offices, Canon Delaney and his parish clerk disappeared through a small brown door marked 'Vestry', only to emerge in suits and ties, looking for all the world like ordinary men. We walked back past a new ship's chandler, a woollen shop, a leather shop and tobacconist, and a small supermarket selling provisions for yachtsmen alongside goods for local residents.

Although serviced by an Anglican chaplain, the Coronarium is multi-denominational. The silver chalice and paten, the plate which holds the bread at communion, were blessed and given to the chapel by the Pope after Canon Delaney and Mr Drew met him in Rome. Methodists, Pentecostalists and Catholic monks have worshipped there. Although the circle of columns was dedicated by Lord Coggan, former Archbishop of Canterbury, and the altar dedicated by Dr Graham Leonard, former Bishop of London, the Coronarium has never been consecrated as an Anglican chapel. It remains the private chapel of the London World Trade Centre, unbound by parish, denominational and even religious boundaries.

As the grey dock light refracted through the multi-faceted exterior, the hint of another dimension broke through with a sudden shaft of sunlight, and I could have sworn that Lazarus shifted slightly in the breeze.

SERVICE TIMES: The eucharist is celebrated at the Coronarium every Thursday at 12.30 p.m.

St Helen Bishopsgate,
then at St Peter's Cornhill
and now at St Andrew's Church
Church office
33 Great St Helen's
LONDON
EC3A 6AP
(Tel: 0171–283 2231 fax 0171–626 0911)

RECTOR: Prebendary Richard Lucas.

ARCHITECTURE: A full-scale restoration is underway at St Helen's Church, due for completion in spring 1996.

SERMON: Testimony by President Richard Nixon's former special counsel, who served seven months in prison after Watergate. An extraordinary witness of life before and after God, and to the transforming power of religious belief.

AFTER-SERVICE CARE: Packed lunches served for £1.80, but fax or telephone order first.

SPIRITUAL HIGH: Intense and uplifting. Churches like St Helen's make working life amid the pressures and terrors of the City a little more bearable.

If ever a church was of no fixed abode, St Helen Bishopsgate has been it. The story of St Helen's tests to the limit the fashionably evangelical belief that a church consists of its people, not its buildings.

We met beneath the Gothic arches of the Guildhall library in the City of London for the weekly Tuesday lunchtime service, which attracts a regular congregation of 450. The building of St Helen's, named after the mother of Constantine, the first Christian Roman emperor, dates from the twelfth century, and the building has been adapted frequently since. It survived the Reformation, the Great Fire of London and the Blitz, but has been closed since being badly damaged by the IRA's Baltic Exchange bombing in the City.

After the bomb the congregations of 650 on Tuesdays and 500 on Sunday night moved to St Botolph without Bishopgate, another of the City's thirty-nine grade I listed churches, only to receive another blow twelve months later. The bomb that then destroyed the medieval church of St Ethelburga also caused serious damage to

St Botolph, which had just had a £500,000 restoration. St Botolph, whose buildings and contents were insured for £200,000 against the threat of terrorist damage, needed as much as £1 million spent on it, and the congregation of St Helen's was homeless once again.

The dazed worshippers were temporarily squeezed into St Peter's Cornhill, which takes 300 at a push, but have since moved into a fully restored St Andrew's church nearby. For popular preachers, the congregation then had to find other premises, such as Guildhall, the headquarters of the Corporation of London. The Sunday evening service at St Peter's has been divided into two, one following the other, to cope.

The star speaker for our service was Charles Colson, a previous winner of the £650,000 Templeton Prize for Progress in Religion. Mr Colson, formerly President Nixon's special counsel, was sent to prison in 1974 for his part in the Watergate scandal. He converted to Christianity and, while inside, conceived the Prison Fellowship, an evangelical ministry that has 50,000 volunteers worldwide, including some in Britain. It was this that won him the Templeton Prize, the world's largest single financial award, bigger than the Nobel awards. And it was singularly appropriate that a man who snatched such a victory from apparent defeat should be the preacher at a church reeling from two shattering setbacks of its own.

The half-hour service, packed full with businessmen and women, medical students, office workers and other young professionals, normally opens with a hymn which is followed by a reading, a prayer and a twenty-minute talk.

Guildhall has no organ in its library, so the hymn was cancelled and we went straight into the prayer and the talk. Mr Colson, a former Marine Corps captain, was a magnetic speaker. 'I know the whole world laughed at my conversion,' he said. 'It kept the cartoonists of America clothed and fed for a month. People wrote the most incredulous stories about the White House tough guy turning to God. Twenty years later, I am more certain of the reality of Jesus Christ than I am of my own reality.' Even though he must have told his story dozens of times before, he managed to make it sound fresh. The educated, intelligent professionals in the audience were evidently wholly convinced by his startling faith. 'The answer to the ethical malaise that is infecting the West is going to be as people come to terms with the living God, [they will] come together in their congregations, lives and witness to the Kingdom of God in the midst of the decay and decadence of culture.' He challenged us to examine our lives. 'If you do not believe in God, what do you believe in? I have discovered in twenty years that there are no atheists. There are only people running away from God, rebelling against the moral truth that is within them.'

In keeping with their devout evangelicalism, worshippers at St Helen's have already been examining their lives and consciences to see what they can learn from the two blows dealt their church by terrorism. The Rev. Hugh Palmer, the curate, said: 'It is helpfully humbling. Before we had our own buildings and resources, and we used to say the church is the people and not the buildings. While that is definitely true, it is not such a glib phrase for us now as it used to be. We say it with no less conviction, but we realise the cost of it.'

SERVICES: Tuesday lunchtime: two services, at 12.35 p.m. (twenty-five minutes) and 1.15 p.m. (thirty minutes); Sunday services: 10.15 a.m. morning worship; Holy Communion first Sunday in the month; evening worship: 6 p.m. and 8 p.m.

St Paul's Cathedral
St Paul's Churchyard
LONDON
EC4M 8AD
(Tel: 0171–248 4619)

DEAN: The Very Rev. Eric Evans.

ARCHITECTURE: Wren's Baroque masterpiece can never fail to astonish even a regular.

SERMON: Entertaining romp backwards through literature, from the *Sun* to Genesis. Further proof that the best of British sermons are to be found in our cathedrals.

MUSIC: Chants sung exquisitely by the all-male choir; even those who knew the settings were content to sit and listen. Fabulous organ playing.

LITURGY: Traditional Book of Common Prayer, made easy by service sheet provided.

AFTER-SERVICE CARE: Might eventually be a cafe in the crypt. Dean made brave attempt to chat to entire congregation plus tourists on the way out.

SPIRITUAL HIGH: Solidity of a rock beneath a dome.

To worship at St Paul's is to experience the Church of England as it was, is now but is unlikely to be for much longer, given the controversy over women priests. Although women deacons assist at services, this is the showpiece for the London diocese, where opposition to women priests in the Church of England is strongest.

It must also be one of the few places where you can enter a tourist attraction and become part of it, comparable perhaps to visiting a museum and becoming one of the exhibits.

At the service I attended, hordes of tourists stared from the back as we sang, prayed and listened to the sermon. Some stood for the entire service, at liberty to join in, but choosing to watch, roped off behind rows of empty seats. As the service progressed, the numbers of watchers increased, adding to the spiritual atmosphere a sensation that we might be nothing more than a religious oddity in a secular age. The non-religious visiting London might be forgiven for counting Wren's construction, completed in 1710, as just another sight to 'do', along with the Tower and Trafalgar Square. It must be easy to forget that cathedrals are primarily centres of worship and mission.

But to attend a service at St Paul's is to step back to a golden age when the voices of choristers soared, liturgies moved the spirit and sermons swayed the nation. St Paul's is at the front line of the battle between God and Mammon. Admission charges were introduced recently and have transformed the cathedral's precarious financial state, although they are not levied on Sundays or for weekday services. A new shop in the crypt will add to the attractions.

Virgers have been redesignated as stewards and virgers (the ancient spelling of virger, unique to St Paul's, has been retained). An evangelical, Michael Saward, has been made a residentiary canon, alongside the traditionalist Anglo-Catholics more usual at St Paul's.

Among Anglo-Catholics, St Paul's is treasured as the only place in England where an Anglican can receive communion from a cardinal. Only a communicant of the Roman Catholic church may receive communion from Cardinal Basil Hume at Westminster Cathedral, so 'wannabe' Catholics in the Church of England go to St Paul's, where two of the three minor canons are cardinals, one the junior and one the senior. The titles, relics of pre-Reformation Roman Catholicism, date from the time of Richard II, and derive from the Latin word *cardo* (hinge).

The chancel is the most richly decorated part of the cathedral, with Grinling Gibbons's oak and limewood carvings, now restored, set off by sparkling mosaics depicting animals, fish and birds in the saucer-shaped domes.

The cathedral is run by the dean (the Very Rev. Eric Evans) and chapter, which consists of a number of residentiary canons (the title given to a clergyman who belongs to a cathedral chapter). The prebendaries belong to the greater chapter, which meets annually and advises the dean and chapter. The most important function of the greater chapter is to elect the Bishop of London, who preaches regularly here.

As we arrived at St Paul's, the peal of twelve bells rang out while dozens of coaches pulled up and hundreds of tourists, hung with Canons of the photographic variety, trooped out and into the cathedral. Our service, matins, followed the traditional rite of the Church of England, with a hymn, chants, lessons, the Creed, prayers, the sermon and a final hymn.

Opposite us, alone on a chair below the stalls, an angel appeared to have descended from the ornate gold-leaf mosaic over the choir vault. The tiny, blond cherub turned out to be a probationer chorister. Probationers start at the age of seven and are admitted to the choir after about twelve months. The ten probationers and twenty-five other choristers are boarders at the choir school at the east end of the cathedral.

St Paul's is not a parish church, and couples who wish to marry there need a special licence from the Archbishop of Canterbury. About 100 people worship here each Sunday, but visitors swell numbers to 500. On feast days, such as Easter, the cathedral attracts many more and can be nearly full.

Each month a different canon is officially 'in residence' and responsible, with the dean, for worship. For our service it was the turn of Canon Christopher Hill who, as precentor, is also in charge of the choir school.

'One of the great privileges of serving here in St Paul's is that in our worship we come from all over the world. Those of you sitting here will probably have as your next door neighbour someone from the other side of the globe. We welcome this morning a group from the Icelandic women's society.'

His sermon, about the passion of Christ, was a literary and spiritual treat, with erudite references to Dostoevsky, William Blake and other writers, interspersed with quotations from the Bible and the *Sun*. Some truths can be expressed only imperfectly in theological prose, Canon Hill said. 'We intuit rather more from the music and poetry of Passiontide.'

Many stayed for the communion that followed, but those of us who left after matins were followed out by the voices of the choir, with the previously blank faces of the tourists registering wonder as the spectacle of the Christian communion service unfolded.

SUNDAY SERVICES: Holy Communion 8 a.m.; matins 10.30 a.m.; Holy Communion 11.30 a.m.; evensong 3.15 p.m. Weekdays (except Sat): matins 7.30 a.m.; Holy Communion 8 a.m. and 12.30 p.m.; evensong 5 p.m.

The Metropolitan Cathedral of the Most Precious Blood
Victoria St
Westminster
LONDON SW1P 1QW
(Tel: 0171–834 7452)

ADMINISTRATOR: Monsignor George Stack.

ARCHITECTURE: Byzantine basilica style built on the site of a large women's prison by John Francis Bentley, who converted to Catholicism in his twenties.

HOMILY: An appeal for service from regular members by Mgr George Stack. 'We must always remember the necessity of building the church before we build a church. The church is made up of living members, you and I, and not dependent on buildings.'

MUSIC: Astonishing sight and sound of men and boys singing fifteenth-century Taverner mass and ancient Gregorian plainchant from the deep apse, with its perfect acoustics, beyond and above the high altar and marble baldachino.

LITURGY: Solemn mass, the normative rite of the Second Vatican Council, combining ancient Latin plainchant with scriptural texts in the vernacular taken from the Jerusalem Bible.

AFTER-SERVICE CARE: Tea, coffee and biscuits in the cathedral hall, a mini-version of the cathedral, also designed by Bentley, and newly restored to its former glory.

SPIRITUAL HIGH: Sacred but accessible solemn mass.

Westminster was deserted but at the cathedral tourists and worshippers strolled in and out of the nave, overflowing on Sunday morning despite its being the highest and widest in the country. Catholics chatted among themselves in a number of western European languages, switched off the video cameras on their shoulders and simultaneously crossed themselves with holy water from the font near the entrance.

Many stopped to examine the leaflets of rosary meditations by the Pope on sale inside before exploring the crowded gift shop, which was doing a brisk trade in CDs of the cathedral choir, rosaries and gold-plated medallions of the Pope.

I lit a votive light, made a donation of 25p as asked and said a quick prayer in the Chapel of the Blessed Sacrament before the solemn mass began. This was one of seven Sunday masses, which include a folk mass, a traditional hymn singing mass, high mass and low mass, attended by 4,500 people in all. There is also morning prayer, sung in English, and solemn vespers with a traditional Benediction in Latin with a full choir in the afternoon.

Nearly all the 1,500 people were dressed smartly, blue and black silk predominating, giving the basilica an Eastern feel. Scaffolding, now gone, in the sanctuary behind the large wooden cross did not detract from the sense of holiness, and Mgr Stack later told me he considered it a 'work of art'.

The bell tolled from the 284-feet slender tower before service began to call us to worship, and organ scholar Gerard Skinner put us in the mood with a magnificent and solemn improvisation on a plainchant which softened as the mass grew closer. A small bell rang solemnly to indicate that mass was about to begin, and the atmosphere changed instantly from one of Mammon and tourism to one of God and worship.

The choir of twenty-six choristers and ten lay clerks in purple and white, followed by eight altar servers, one carrying the book of the Gospels, processed through to the sanctuary, followed by Mgr Stack in vestments, the liturgical colour being green to symbolise an ordinary Sunday of the church's year. As a sign of honour Mgr Stack censed the altar, a symbol of the presence of Christ, and welcomed visitors. He went on to bless the water, a symbol of baptism, and salt, a symbol of zest and taste for new life.

The enchantment of hearing the choir singing the Credo in Latin plainchant remained with me long after the service.

This was the stuff of everyday worship at the cathedral, which in 1995 ran a year-long programme of events to mark the 100th anniversary of its foundation.

Volunteers are needed, from sacred metal polishers to bereavement counsellors. Mgr Stack asked us 'to reflect on what you can do to carry the mission of this cathedral forward'.

SERVICE TIMES: call 0171–828 4732.

St Mary the Virgin
30 Bourne St
LONDON
SW1W 8JJ
(Tel: 0171–730 2423)

VICAR: The Rev. William Scott.

ARCHITECTURE: A poor example of Victorian Gothic revivalism, although the many changes since it was built in 1874, including a Martin Travers reredos, give the feel of a Renaissance church with baroque additions.

SERMON: Guest preacher delivered thoughtful homily on Christ's compassion.

MUSIC: Mass by Lassus, the classic Renaissance composer. Beautiful choral endeavours from the choir aloft.

LITURGY: A tantalising mixture which defies any of the usual pigeonholes of traditional, modern, Anglican or Catholic.

AFTER-SERVICE CARE: Mineral water or wine in the presbytery, and the chance to meet some wonderful English eccentrics.

SPIRITUAL HIGH: Arguably more Roman than the Romans.

Although the words Church of England are clearly marked on the noticeboard of St Mary's, Bourne Street, in London, an unobservant passer-by might easily mistake it for a Roman Catholic church. But for a person to do so, and perhaps make his or her way instead to the evangelical St Michael's Chester Square around the corner, would be to miss an experience of worship which many believe today is endangered.

St Mary's is a leading light in the Anglo-Catholic or high church wing of Anglicanism. It is one of the few churches which can be described with some justification as traditionalist, or more Roman than the Romans. The board outside, on a discreet red-brick Victorian exterior typical of Catholic churches built in the last century, advertises Mass, not Holy Communion. The Rev. Bill Scott is known as the parish priest, not the vicar, and is addressed by all as 'father'.

Anglo-Catholicism grew out of the Oxford Movement, begun in 1833 by John Henry Newman, John Keble and Edward Pusey to defend the Church of England against the prevailing extremes of Protestantism and Romanism. After an internal struggle which, in many ways, mirrors today's debate about women priests, Newman began to doubt the claims of the Anglican church and became a Roman Catholic in 1845, leaving Pusey and Keble as the 'movement' leaders.

Many Anglo-Catholics believe the vote to ordain women priests was the death knell for the Oxford Movement. Some of these are contemplating following Newman down the difficult road to Rome. But worship at St Mary's, where debate about women priests is muted, should convince many that not only will it take a lot more than a controversial decision by the General Synod to put an end to Anglo-Catholicism, but the church might even be strengthened as a result.

As if in sympathy with the upheavals testing the very foundations of the traditionalist wing of the church, St Mary's shuddered repeatedly during our worship, as London Underground trains rattled underneath. In the porch, a copy of a 1989 joint declaration by the former Archbishop of Canterbury, Dr Robert Runcie, and Pope John Paul II, advocates the pursual of the arduous journey to Christian unity, 'whatever obstacles are perceived to block the path'. No amount of juddering can shake it from the wall. Books on sale include some published from Faith House in Westminster, from where the response of the opponents to women priests is co-ordinated by the umbrella group Forward in Faith.

At St Mary's, worshippers have one thing in common: a love of tradition and of the sacraments, such as communion, penance and baptism. According to the Catholic Media Office in London, High Mass and Low Mass no longer exist in the Roman Catholic Church, and there is only Mass. Sung Mass at Catholic churches is often referred to colloquially as High Mass, however, and in the Anglo-Catholic wing of the Church of England, High Mass is a thriving institution, a heady feast of song, incense and ritual.

The service was based on the traditional Anglican rite for communion, with additions from the Roman missal. The church seemed full, with about 150 people. Worshippers included Augustine Hoey, a world-famous missionary, and Alan Porter, manager of Wippell, the clerical outfitters.

The service opened with the introit procession, with clergy, laymen and altar servers bearing a cross and candles, and waving a silver censer. One of the servers turned out to be Gordon Dulieu, communications officer for the liberally inclined, pro-women priests Southwark diocese across the river. The three men leading the worship assumed different roles, indicated by their dress. Fr Scott was in the role of deacon and wore a gold silk dalmatic, diaconal equivalent of the chasuble, over a white linen and lace alb. The celebrant was the Rev. David Priest, a non-stipendiary clergyman, whose full-time job is group manager for the St Mungo community trust, an organisation in Fulham that looks after people who come out of psychiatric hospitals. He wore a gold silk chasuble over an alb. Michael Mundy, who as a layman was the representative of the congregation, wore a gold silk tunicle over an alb. All three wore birettas, a square cap worn normally by Roman Catholic clergy.

At the 'Gloria in Excelsis', which was in Latin, the three men sat down and removed their birettas in unison. My neighbour Elizabeth Mills, who led Women Against the Ordination of Women, explained: 'Birettas come off at the name of Jesus.' (Since my visit, Augustine Hoey, Gordon Dulieu, David Priest and Elizabeth Mills have all changed their ecclesiastical allegiance.) The Gospel, wrapped in a gold silken tasselled cover, was then brought in procession to the lectern and censed. A guest speaker, Fr Alan Grainge, preached on Christ's compassion. 'We are loved as we are,' he intoned from a pulpit that reached high above us. 'God longs for us to become better people, to be the people that he intends. But he loves us here and now, as we are.' At the end we sang the 'Regina Caeli', an anthem in honour of Mary, mother of Jesus, and a traditional extra in this church. As we sipped drinks in the presbytery after the service, the fear that women priests will mean an end to Anglo-Catholicism seemed to slip away. It is impossible to imagine St Mary's moving into the Roman Catholic Church today, modernised as it has been by the second Vatican Council (1962–65). In its Anglo-Catholic extremity, St Mary's remains immutably Anglican and at the same time reassuringly Catholic, witness to hope for the Church of England.

SUNDAY SERVICES: Low Mass 9 a.m., 9.45 a.m., 7 p.m. High Mass 11 a.m. Solemn evensong and Benediction 6 p.m.

Musama Disco Christo Church, the Methodist Church
Mostyn Road
Brixton
South London
UK office
40 Brailsford Road
LONDON
SW2 2TE
(Tel: 0181-674 3999)

PASTOR: Rev. Jerisdan Hartnah Jehu-Appiah.
ARCHITECTURE: Modern, red-brick building.
SERMON: Fiery, with useful pastoral advice.
MUSIC: Exotic and tuneful.
LITURGY: Just say 'amen' after every alleluia.
AFTER-SERVICE CARE: Tea and coffee, counselling available.
SPIRITUAL HIGH: An enlivening beat.

To an African-style drum beat and shaking tambourines and akassas, or rattling gourds, London's black Ghanaian pentecostal Christian community dances each Sunday away in Brixton. Like so many small, inner-city churches, the Musama Disco Christo Church is a triumph of hope against adversity. The unremarkable red-brick, modern building, borrowed each week from its Methodist owners, stands like some strange missionary outpost amid dismal housing estates.

The church itself reverses the historical British view of white missionaries who attempt to convert the dark continent to Christianity. Here we have a black African church offering Christian witness amid a secular English atheism of the most despairing kind. It is one of the thriving black-led pentecostal churches which are growing as fast as other churches decline. With their lively Christian witness in the bleak urban landscape, churches like this provide spiritual homes for the hundreds of black people who feel discriminated against in the predominantly white mainstream churches.

The word 'discotheque' was in use in Britain as long ago as 1951, according to the *Oxford English Dictionary*, which defines it as a club, etc, where recorded music is played for dancing. But the use of the word 'disco' by the Musama Disco Christo Church pre-dates this by thirty years. It was founded in Ghana in 1919 by Pastor Jerisdan Jehu-Appiah's grandfather, Jemisimiham, and has grown into a sizeable indigenous West African pentecostal church, with more than 100,000 members.

Pastor Jeri, as he is called, came to Britain in 1979 to minister to the immigrant pentecostal Ghanaian community. 'It is called the Disco Church, but that has nothing to do with discos as we understand them today,' he says. 'The full name and its translation was given by charismatic inspiration to the founder.' Disco in this context means The Army of the Cross of Christ. The initials MDCC are engraved on the altar cross in the church.

Nevertheless, it is a place where disco lovers can express themselves in an appropriate and reverent manner with dance, music and devout prayer. Like most pentecostalists and charismatics, members of the Musama Disco Christo Church receive the 'gifts of the spirit', or charisms, listed by St Paul in 1 Corinthians 12–14. These include the gifts of healing, prophecy, wisdom, faith, speaking in tongues and interpretation.

The liturgy at first seemed unstructured, interspersed with impromptu 'alleluia, amens', but it emerged that the service followed a series of prayers Pastor Jeri had written. From the hymn book, *Songs of Inspiration*, also largely written by him, we sang African and modern gospel songs, augmented by spine-tingling African harmonies from the congregation.

The pastor's work has a growing following, and is occasionally performed publicly by children and the younger church members in his black choir, Voices of Inspiration.

Pastor Jeri works in his spare time as a chaplain and pastoral counsellor at the Maudsley Hospital in Denmark Hill, south London. He leads regular healing services, group meetings and Bible studies at his home, which attract many people from the wider community, plus members of the 120-strong church. His job-search group has sometimes temporarily put itself out of work by finding jobs for all its members, but is at present in action again through a branch of the church which gives guidance in areas of homelessness, employment, mental health and marriage.

Ghanaians and Afro-Caribbeans travel to Brixton from all over greater London for these groups and the two-and-a-half hour Sunday service, which seemed to pass in a few minutes when we were there. This was in spite of a sermon which lasted half an hour and announcements which extended it even further. The pastor believes there is an art to preaching, and watching him was better

than seeing some West End performers. Crescendos and diminu-
endos, shouting, pointing and dramatic gesticulations accompanied
his Bible-based commentaries. He uses a microphone, but does not
really need it. Sometimes he brings in a drama group to act out the
sermon for him, other times he will act it out himself. Unlike many
preachers, he is not afraid to address the issue of the devil and the
nature of evil.

> One day, I was talking to a man who asked: 'Can I be a devil?'
> I said: 'No, you can't. Everyone has evil tendencies in them but
> I don't think that means you become a devil, because Satan is
> an entity in himself. Why do you ask?' He replied: 'Sometimes
> I feel so angry that I find only evil going on in my head. That's
> when I feel that maybe I have turned into a devil.' Don't we
> sometimes feel so much anger in us, so much hatred in us, that
> all the good disappears? This might not be caused by the devil,
> but by life's circumstances: poverty, troubles and hardship.
> Difficulties will come. But in all this we need to remember,
> these troubles will not finish us.'

To his left sat his wife, Cynthia, who leads the church prayer
group, and to his right the church elder, a layman. All three
wore vivid white cassocks, reflecting light on to the white lace
headscarves of women in the congregation. Women have risen to
be among the most senior evangelists in the organisation. None in
England celebrates Holy Communion, but the church is not, in any
case, particularly sacramental. The eucharist services are reserved
for Christian festivals and holidays. At the end of services, personal
testimony and prayers are invited from the congregation. Anyone
who believes pentecostal Christianity to be facile, or to offer easy
answers, needs only hear the testimonies to have such prejudice
confounded.

SUNDAY SERVICES: Mostyn Road 3–5.30 p.m. Group meet-
    ings, Tues and Wed; healing service, Thurs evenings; Bible
    study, Fri evening all at Brailsford Road.

VICAR: The Rev. Sandy Millar.

ARCHITECTURE: Commissioners' Gothic-style, with an attractive Victorian interior. Since my visit the wooden pews have been removed, replaced by chairs and carpet, and a lovely pink coat of paint applied in places.

SERMON: Well-delivered biblical exposition on why God loves people who give lots of money away.

MUSIC: Rousing songs led by a Christian rock band. Enjoyable, but might seem startling to those more used to *Hymns Ancient and Modern*.

LIGURGY: Barely evident, but what there was seemed to be adapted well from the modern material available in the Church of England, largely due to an injection of evangelical spirituality.

AFTER-SERVICE CARE: Coffee and orange juice, but no tea. Youngsters chat among themselves, exuding post-service glow.

SPIRITUAL HIGH: Heady cocktail of worship, prayer and healing.

Holy Trinity Brompton is known in the trade as HTB, rather as the Archbishop of Canterbury is the ABC. HTB is full of DCCs, deeply committed Christians, who have the effect of making ordinary Anglicans hesitate to call themselves Christian at all. The church is the butt of frequent jokes and arouses hostility among those who fear its appeal. Yet Holy Trinity is one of the most popular and successful churches in London, overflowing with worshippers, and regularly 'plants' or starts new congregations. Offshoots are thriving in Battersea, Kensington and nearby Onslow Square and there has been at least one other new church plant. There is barely room for the present number of Sunday worshippers, almost 1,500. Clergy are looking for another church in which to plant a new congregation.

We attended the informal evening service of worship and

teaching, with a healing session at the end. Because it was the third Sunday of the month, we celebrated communion. Hundreds of youthful, fresh-faced adherents, eyes gleaming with the light of salvation, raised their hands and danced to the rock beat that underlay nearly every hymn. Emotions ran high. One woman was sobbing before the service had even begun.

Eight television monitors posted above the wooden pews allowed even those of us hiding away at the back to see clearly every gesture of the vicar, Sandy Millar, who opened the service with prayers for all those going through difficult emotional experiences in families and the community. We prayed for peace, for the church and for its leader. We listened to a reading from St Paul's second letter to the Corinthians about how much God loves a cheerful giver. So far, it seemed relatively normal.

But then the drums and guitars were struck, we were urged to 'get a little bit of rhythm going', and the service took off with four or five songs in quick succession.

It is easy to mock churches like Holy Trinity, but the sermon that ensued was one of the most effective I have heard. If all churches used the technique of curate Nicky Gumbel in canvassing for funds, the Church of England might not be in its present financial predicament. The collection plates had already gone round, so Mr Gumbel could let himself go without fear of resentment.

Like God issuing the Ten Commandments to Moses on Mount Sinai, he listed ten powerful reasons for generous giving, alluding to biblical texts. 'Whoever sows sparingly will also reap sparingly,' he warned. I began to regret my 50p in the collection. 'Whoever sows generously will also reap generously.' He admitted a certain reluctance among clergy to speak about money at all.

'We think if we talk about it, we will never see people again. But Jesus was not reluctant to talk about money.' His sermon evinced a feature common to most evangelical churches: having rejected the biblical criticism which has questioned the veracity of so many Christian texts, their clergy still treat what Jesus said as literal truth.

'Generous giving transforms our characters,' he said. 'Generous giving meets genuine needs.' Holy Trinity has its own tabloid newspaper, *HTB in Focus*. One twelve-page edition reports that sermons such as this, culminating in a 'gift day', resulted in pledges amounting to £225,000. This goes towards the £250,000 refit of the church, which involves replacing the pews with carpets and chairs. It will also help the £150,000 needed for the church's activities in the coming year.

We did not say a confession but prayed while Mr Millar confessed on our behalf.

For the communion, the Anglican liturgy was reduced to its minimum. We did not kneel at the altar or drink from the cup but took communion standing up, some dipping their wafer in the wine as we had been invited to do.

The formal part of the service was then closed, but we were asked to stand and open ourselves to 'the spirit of God', the prelude to a healing ceremony. Mr Millar appealed for those in pain to come forward. At first, none responded. 'There are a number of people here with pain in their chest,' he said. 'I just want to see if anyone responds to that. Anyone got a pain in their chest? Someone with a sharp pain in the back of the neck? Anyone here at all?' He moved on to tooth pains and marital problems. Those brave enough to venture to the front were prayed over and ministered to. The rest of us went to the crypt downstairs for goodbyes. We left, and I regretted only that he had not mentioned earache.

SUNDAY SERVICES: Traditional sung communion 9 a.m.; informal worship and teaching, followed by healing 11 a.m.; informal worship and teaching, with communion on the third Sunday of the month and healing prayers 6.30 p.m.

**The Russian Orthodox Cathedral of the Dormition of
the Mother of God and All the Saints
67 Ennismore Gardens
LONDON
SW7 1NH
(Tel: 0171–584 0096)**

CLERGY: The Most Rev. Metropolitan Anthony of Sourozh, The Right Rev. Archbishop Anatoly of Kerch, Fr Michael Fortounatto, Fr Alexander Fostiropoulos, Fr John Lee.

ARCHITECTURE: Early Christian basilica-style, built in 1849 by Lewis Vulliamy.

SERMON: Impressively good sermon by Archbishop Anatoly, considering at the time he had been in this country for little more than a year. Metropolitan Anthony's justly celebrated sermons are invariably short.

MUSIC: Early medieval chants, such as the Kiev chant, harmonised by nineteenth- and twentieth-century composers and performed by the cathedral's large and renowned mixed choir standing in a gallery. The most beautiful chant, the Beatitudes from Christ's Sermon on the Mount, was sung to a harmonisation of an ancient chant used by blind pilgrims.

LITURGY: Usually that of St John Chrysostom, a teaching saint in Orthodoxy, but on this occasion, since it was Lent, it was that of St Basil the Great. Both date from the fourth century, although the wordings and ritual of both have undergone various modifications since then. On the second Sunday in the month, the Liturgy is celebrated mainly in English.

AFTER-SERVICE CARE: At the end of the service, non-Orthodox may receive, if they wish, the *antidoron*, which is blessed but not consecrated bread. Free tea and biscuits are served in the new hall complex, and as well as books, the shop sells a wide selection of music and icons.

SPIRITUAL HIGH: Enlightening and instructive.

Orthodoxy means right belief and right worship. The emphasis in Orthodoxy is on love, the greatest of the three graces listed by St Paul. And the love shown at this cathedral is proof that love works. This is one church in Britain where the congregation is growing by the week, with increasing numbers, not only of Russians who travel to the West and return to their ancient faith but also of many other nationalities.

In Britain, the Orthodox include Greek, Russian, Serbian, Romanian, Bulgarian, Antiochian and members of the Oriental churches, with a total membership of 275,000 to 300,000.

I attended the cathedral church of the Russian Orthodox diocese of Sourozh, which covers the British Isles and has about 3,000 members. The diocese comes under the spiritual jurisdiction of Patriarch Alexis of Moscow and All Russia. The worldwide Orthodox church consists of a number of self-governing churches, although all acknowledge the honorary primacy of the Patriarch of Constantinople, along with the three other ancient patriarchates of Alexandria, Antioch and Jerusalem.

The service lasted about two hours, and for much of it the members of the 200-strong congregation stood, bowed and occasionally prostrated themselves in veneration. Irina Kirillova, a member of the diocesan assembly and parish council, said: 'It is a good Orthodox principle that you are transported on to another level of being and you forget about time.' Orthodox churches never have pews, because the Orthodox position of prayer is standing and because pews inhibit freedom of worship and impede the various processions. Chairs were supplied for those who find standing difficult. The number who remained standing throughout was impressive, considering the strict adherence by Orthodox Christians to their Lenten fast. The forty days of Lent, which we were in the midst of, are calculated slightly differently than in the Western churches, so that Lent begins seven full weeks before Easter Sunday. During this period, meat, fish, dairy products, olive oil and alcohol are normally not eaten or drunk. Most of those present were keeping this fast, and the slow, sad rhythm of our service was a sign of the Lenten mood, in preparation for the feast of Easter.

The service was celebrated by Archbishop Anatoly of Kerch, who came to England in December 1991 to minister to the influx of Russians that followed Yeltsin's accession to power. He arrived fresh from work with Orthodox Christians living in some tension among the Muslim Tartars of Ufa, southwest of the Urals. His understated style of worship is complemented by an amazed sparkle in his eyes, suggesting astonishment at the changes that have brought him to the West and freed the Russian Church from repression in the East.

Before the service began, the bookshop did a brisk trade. The cathedral shop is now housed in enlarged premises in the new hall complex adjoining the cathedral, and has a comprehensive list of books on all aspects of Orthodoxy, in both English and Russian.

Many of the Russians arriving here have a deep faith but little knowledge of their church, and are reading avidly. Catechetical classes have been laid on to help them. Father Alexander Fostiropoulos, the Orthodox chaplain at London University, took confessions in open church before and during the service, as is Orthodox practice.

In the Orthodox church, parish clergy are married but future priests must marry before they are ordained. Bishops are taken from the monastic clergy, and are therefore celibate at the time of their episcopacy, although widowed parish priests can take monastic vows and become bishops. Bishop Basil of Sergievo, from the Oxford parish and one of four presidents of the ecumenical organisation, Churches Together in England, is a widower. The word 'liturgy' means common work, and we were technically concelebrating with the priest. As a congregation we 'prayed' the words of the Liturgy, and visibly took part by making the sign of the cross as an 'amen' to prayers. The Liturgy followed a pattern similar to non-Orthodox churches, with psalms, epistle and Gospel readings followed by the Creed, the consecration of the bread and wine, the Lord's Prayer and the communion. The sermon, which should be preached after the Gospel, is often in parish practice placed near the end of the service, as this one was. Archbishop Anatoly wore black, the symbolic colour for Lent, although the next day after my visit he would have celebrated in white because the Orthodox churches that year celebrated Easter one week after most other churches, since they calculate the date using the old (Julian) calendar. The archbishop's robes, crowned by a jewelled mitre, were ornate and glistened with silver, the sign that he is Christ's representative.

Eastern and western Christendom have been estranged formally since 1054, when three legates of Pope Leo IX placed a bull of excommunication against the Easterns on the altar of St Sophia in Constantinople, one of the most beautiful churches in the world, which became a mosque after the city fell to the Turks in 1453. After centuries of doctrinal debate, the excommunication was the final breach marking a great schism.

The schism centred on a phrase in the Creed, the filioque, meaning 'and the son', which refers to the idea that the Holy Ghost proceeds from the father and the son. The filioque was added to the Nicene Creed in the sixth century and adopted at Rome soon after the year 1000, in spite of persistent opposition from the East. But the two were already divided over Papal claims. The Roman church saw itself as the centre of unity for entire Christendom, while the eastern Christians believed the Church consisted of five patriarchates, including Rome, all of equal status and all equally based. In a revised edition of his standard work on the Orthodox Church, Bishop Kallistos (Timothy) Ware, a fellow of Pembroke College, Oxford, and Greek Orthodox Bishop of Diokleia, refers to the primacy of the sacraments in worship. 'Orthodoxy rejects any attempt to diminish the materiality of the sacraments,' he says. The Orthodox believe in *metousiosis*, that during the consecration the bread and wine become the body and blood of Christ. The Orthodox avoid the use of the Catholic term, transubstantiation, to describe this process.

At the service I attended, mysticism and symbolism were central to the Liturgy, delivered in English and Church Slavonic, a somewhat archaic form of the vernacular. Prayers for the Queen, royal family and government were in English, and the Beatitudes from Christ's Sermon on the Mount sung in Slavonic to an old chant.

A small relic of the venerated ninth-century patriarch, Paul of Constantinople, was brought to England from Mount Athos by the choirmaster, Father Michael, and has been incorporated into the altar, set behind the *iconostasis*, or icon screen. Over the altar burn *lampada*, wicks in oil, symbolising prayers of supplication or intercession. The icon screen represents a window on to the transfigured world of the risen Christ in the sanctuary, and is beneath the half dome at the end of the whitewashed church. Each wall was hung with many icons, most with candles or oil lamps before them. The church also has relics of several other saints in the cathedral, and venerates the early saints of the British Isles, such as Cuthbert and Alban.

Among the worshippers were a mother and daughter from Bulgaria and two Serbian women wearing headscarves. Two-thirds of the congregation were English converts and their descendants. There were many people of other nationalities and backgrounds.

Before the service the icons were censed, with clouds of incense from a thurible on a long chain. The sanctuary was censed often during the service, and the congregation was censed before the beginning of the service, before the reading of the Gospel and before the Great Entrance. Worshippers often crossed themselves, from right to left, the opposite to other Churches. The congregation received communion standing. Children can receive communion from baptism. They go to their first confession at about seven years old, when they begin to be aware of the concept of sin.

The archbishop began his sermon with 'Dear brothers and sisters', and asked us to think about the meaning the Church puts into its Lenten services.

It would be easy to think of this church, near to Harrods, behind the Roman Catholics' Brompton Oratory and the Anglicans' Holy Trinity, as an exotic import from the East bearing little relation to traditional British Christianity. But after these hours of concentration on mystery, with nothing to say but much to think about, Orthodoxy seemed instead an embodiment of the universal spirit of Christianity as it was from the beginning.

SUNDAY SERVICES: Liturgy 10.30 a.m.

The Shaftesbury Society
Shaftesbury Christian Centre
2 Austin Road
LONDON
SW11 5JP
(Tel: 0171–622 4360)

PASTOR: Tony Powell.

ARCHITECTURE: Nondescript modern building, but infinitely preferable to the hideous high-rise blocks around it.

SERMONS: Two. Entertaining testimony from ice skater Nicky Slater, after which the pastor preached on the Christian inheritance.

MUSIC: Standard, lively evangelical fare from young musicians on guitars and tambourines.

LITURGY: Virtually non-existent.

AFTER-SERVICE CARE: Coffee, orange juice and as much pastoral care as anyone could ask for.

SPIRITUAL HIGH: Considerable, particularly mid-service.

At first I mistook this church for a pub. The low, red-brick building and the sign outside, 'The Shaftesbury', has led others to make the same mistake. At least one passer-by looking for a drink has strayed in, and was tempted to stay by the more ethereal spirit on offer. I was met at the door by Ruth Powell, the pastor's wife. She and her husband Tony have been there for nearly twenty years and, in keeping with the tradition of the Shaftesbury Society, vacated their rambling presbytery so it could become a medical centre, and now live in a council house nearby.

The Shaftesbury Society began life as the Ragged School Union in 1844, and was renamed in 1914 after its founder, the social reformer, the 7th Earl of Shaftesbury, to whom the Eros statue in London's Piccadilly was erected as a memorial in 1893. The society has become one of Britain's leading Christian social welfare charities, providing education and care for people with disabilities, the homeless and the elderly.

The Shaftesbury Christian Centre, one of fifty churches attached to the society, has close links with the Beth Shalom drug rehabilitation centre near Clapham Common in south London. The centre was set up a hundred years ago by the Bible preacher John Dyer, who took hundreds of children crippled by rickets on their first outings to the seaside. The children at our service appeared wonderfully healthy in comparison. Rounded children and babies played on the floor as the three vocalists in the pop group led us in 'Rejoice in the Lord', a popular evangelical song.

The church was filled with people of all ages and many ethnic groups, most dressed in bright colours and smiling in the manner of those ecstatic Christians for whom church is the highpoint and not the penance of the week.

Pastor Tony Powell, one of four church elders, began: 'Lord, for this day given to us, a day that we can spend in worship, we give you thanks.' We moved into 'Blessed Be the Name of the Lord'. 'Just keep on praising him,' the worship leader Mick Richardson urged, as my neighbours closed their eyes, swayed their bodies and clapped. 'Don't worry about what you look like. Just worship Jesus.' The service was nearly two hours long and had two sermons.

The first was a talk, billed as a 'testimony', from the former ice skater Nicky Slater, whom I last encountered at an ice rink in west London, where he taught me to quickstep. He has abandoned his skating career and is now communications and marketing director for the Shaftesbury Society. He told us how he and his partner Karen Barber became British ice dance champions after Torvill and Dean turned professional. But his skating career ended when he fell in competition, injuring himself.

He converted to Christianity, he and Karen Barber split up, and Mr Slater entered his 'wilderness years'. He introduced us to Doris, a dummy with a pink sequin skating dress and green hair, with whom he did a couple of exhibitions. 'She helped me through my wilderness years.' His breakthrough came, he said, when he joined the Shaftesbury Society. 'You can make a difference to the world around you, even when times are tough. God has got a plan for you,' he said. 'We aim to witness to our Christian faith through the work we do rather than by preaching to people.' The children then disappeared to Sunday School, and after some more singing, we settled for sermon number two, from Tony Powell. 'We can be so absorbed in life and all its pressures that the kingdom of God passes us by,' he said. After coffee I left, spiritually satiated, and in no need of added refreshment from the real pub opposite.

SUNDAY SERVICE: family worship 11 a.m.

The Assemblies of the First Born
St Stephen's Church
Battersea Bridge Road and Kersley Street
LONDON SW11 3AD
(Tel: 0171–223 3099)

OVERSEER: The Rev. Charles Wright.
ARCHITECTURE: Victorian.
SERMON: An elucidation of why we should 'praise the Lord', interspersed with many 'Alleluias'.
MUSIC: Enthusiastic gospel soul from choir and individuals, accompanied by young musicians on percussion and electric organ.
LITURGY: Structured loosely around readings, Bible and song.
SPIRITUAL HIGH: The kind of foot-tapping worship that leaves you wanting more.

The young evangelist Carl Napier stood to address us. 'If there is anyone sat here who does not know the Lord Jesus Christ, who had a terrible time in 1993, I am telling you there is hope in the Lord Jesus Christ. Life must go on,' he said, raising his right hand in the air and bursting into an unaccompanied solo. 'Blessed hope, blessed rest for our soul,' he sang, lingering on the last word in a manner that inspired many of the congregation to raise their hands and join in.

Unlike the predominantly white mainstream churches, black churches are growing rapidly in Britain. Many were founded after the Second World War by first or second-generation immigrants, who felt unwelcome in the mainstream churches. Members today include people of all ethnic origins. The Assemblies of the First Born Church just across Battersea Bridge in south London is one of a number of burgeoning black pentecostal churches in Britain. Taking its name from Hebrews 12:23, 'the full concourse and assembly of the firstborn who are enrolled in heaven', it was officially founded in 1961 in Derby, but the Rev. Charles Wright, general overseer for the church in Britain and America, was holding weekly prayer meetings in Battersea as early as 1958.

The four early churches have grown to twenty, and six have been founded in America. The church boasts more than 118 ministers, evangelists, deacons, mothers' pastoral counsellors and missionaries, and there are nearly 200 ordinary members at Battersea alone, plus dozens of children.

On entering I was given a copy of *Redemption Songs*, a collection of 1,000 hymns and choruses, but this was little help as many of the gospel-style songs which filled the next ninety minutes seemed either to be extemporised or known by heart by most of the people there.

The church appeared at first to be nothing out of the ordinary. But as musicians began warming up on the drums and electric organ, the building began to fill with enthusiastic pentecostalists, most of Jamaican origin but now living in southwest London.

Pastor Curtis Sinclair, a young minister, was in the pulpit in front of the chancel. We said alternate verses in a reading from Ephesians and he gave a brief homily. 'Our society is going away from the principles that we have cherished over the years. But I am glad to know, brothers and sisters, there is hope yet. Praise the name of the Lord. Alleluia.' Mr Sinclair continued: 'They need God. Those who know Christ know that this is the answer for the world today. Praise the name of the Lord. Praise the name of God.' Again the congregation followed, growing in ecstasy with each alleluia.

This was the cue for a woman in the congregation to break into song. 'How great is our God,' she began, her powerful voice lifting to the wooden rafters. The musicians picked up the melody and the congregation joined in.

We were invited to 'worship the Lord with our offering', and the collection plate went around. A special collection was made for a new project, to provide food, blankets and clothing for the homeless in central London.

Mr Wright took over to preach. 'Many people went to bed last night. They did not wake up this morning. But we did. Praise the name of the Lord,' he said. 'Do you believe that He can do great things?' he asked. 'Yes,' shouted his congregation.

Singing and dancing continued to the end, and outside the passers-by on their way to and from Chelsea quickened their steps in time to the Caribbean beat now emanating from within the otherwise unremarkable London stocks.

SUNDAY SERVICE: 11.30 a.m. to 1.30 p.m.

Southwest London Vineyard
Elliott School
Pullman Gardens
Putney
LONDON
SW15 3DG
(Tel: 0181-545 0300)

SENIOR PASTOR: John Mumford.
ARCHITECTURE: Brick, glass and concrete school.
SERMON: Mr Mumford spoke on marriage, divorce and the death of love.
MUSIC: Christian pop.
AFTER-SERVICE CARE: Climb over prostrate bodies to reach tea and coffee.
SPIRITUAL HIGH: Dizzyingly stratospheric.

The young man in Doc Martens, jeans and T-shirt was badly hung over. As he spoke it became clear that the previous night's intoxication was induced by a different kind of spirit from that which comes in bottles.

Over the next two hours. I was to see several hundred more become 'drunk in the spirit', laughing, weeping and crying out, many shaking as if in delirium tremens, others simply fainting on the floor. Church leaders, anxious not to embarrass members, insisted we did not photograph the phenomena we witnessed and restricted our access to the first ten minutes.

This unprepossessing school in southwest London suburbia had become one of the first churches in Britain to witness a wave of bizarre spiritual phenomena which is taking on the characteristics of a centennial revival akin to that of the late eighteenth century. The faintings and hysterical laughter, known as being 'slain by the spirit', have attained wider significance more recently since they spread to the established church. Such phenomena are being compared in the country's fast-growing charismatic Christian community to the 'rushing mighty wind' which struck the disciples on the day of Pentecost. They began speaking in tongues and the Apostle Peter stood to say: 'These are not drunken, as ye suppose, seeing it is but the third hour of the day.' Charismatic gifts have appeared in the Church from its beginnings and have been common in some British churches on the fringes, and in places where worship is less formal than here, such as the American South and parts of Africa.

This outbreak began in another branch of the Vineyard fellowship, the Airport Church in Toronto, from which reports had emerged of hundreds of people rocking on their feet and rolling around on the floor for sometimes hours at a time.

As the band began to play and our service rolled into action, the first to raise her hands in the air and begin swaying was Eleanor Mumford, wife of the Putney church's senior pastor, John Mumford. It was Mrs Mumford who visited the Toronto church because she felt 'spiritually bankrupt'. She claimed a 'fantastic' experience and returned to England to pray with her colleagues. She appears to have caused an almost instant ripple effect, with ministers who heard her speak returning to their own churches and inspiring similar phenomena iin what has become known as the 'Toronto Blessing'.

By the second number people were dancing in the aisles, and the back of the young man in front of me had begun vibrating as the beginning of a progression to spiritual drunkenness that was to end in rigid, on-the-spot shaking and leaping.

The Putney church is affiliated to the Association of Vineyard Churches, which has more than 550 churches worldwide. The fellowship, a pioneer in the use of Christian rock and pop music in mainstream churches, was founded in 1978 by the American evangelist John Wimber, the rock singer responsible for the Righteous Brothers. Mr Wimber attracts thousands to prayer and worship meetings when he visits Britain. This church, founded several years ago by Mr Mumford, was the first of its kind in Britain. They practise 'church planting', whereby members leave and found new churches.

After his sermon, Mr Mumford prayed for 'the tornado to visit the church'. The band struck up with the song 'Pour Out Your Spirit'. Outside it was calm, but suddenly the curtains shielding an open door blew in and over my face a huge wind rushed in, scattering service sheets and papers. Alarmed, I started singing along with the band, while nearly everyone else fell over, stood rigid or shaking, sobbing, clutching at their faces or waving their hands before them. I looked back beyond the empty chairs and bodies strewn over the floor, to see many who were not affected were chatting calmly over coffee as if nothing was happening, while bodies lay splayed at their feet, bearing beatific smiles and looks of tremendous peace.

I clambered over a couple of prostrate bodies for tea and coffee, and found myself giggling uncontrollably. Turning to look back at the band, the hall took on a bizarrely infinite perspective. I felt dizzy, grasped a chair in order not to collapse, and recalled that I still had a day's work to do at the office. Recognising I could not at this point afford to be slain by the spirit, I opted instead for spiritual sobriety and a hasty exit, my hands shaking only slightly as I downed the coffee and ran.

SUNDAY SERVICES: 11 a.m. and 6.30 p.m.

Bethel Gospel Standard Strict Baptist Chapel
Chapel Street
LUTON
Bedfordshire
(Tel: 01582 26042)

PASTOR: B.A. Ramsbottom.

ARCHITECTURE: Built 1906 in the plain chapel style typical of its era, with seating for nearly 200, pews and gallery.

MUSIC: Solemn hymns accompanied by deliciously lugubrious organist.

LITURGY: Hymn, reading, prayer, notices, hymn, sermon, hymn.

SERMON: Immensely long at forty-five minutes, but thought-provoking in its exposition of innate sin.

AFTER-SERVICE CARE: Congregation depart for lunch with their families, and invite any visitors who are away from home to go with them.

SPIRITUAL HIGH: Sombre.

The service was about nothing but sin and salvation, yet rarely can a congregation have looked so wholesome, clean, refreshed and at peace during a ninety-minute service as did these Strict Baptists in their small chapel in an old side street in Luton, Bedfordshire.

'We pray that Thou wilt have mercy on England and stem the tide of iniquity and infidelity and immorality,' intoned the pastor, Mr Ramsbottom, who is known by his initials, B.A. 'Leave us not, neither forsake us, O God of our salvation.' A beautiful young woman in a flowery dress and with long, brown hair smiled at me, her head bowed beneath her straw hat.

'May they [the young] realise the vanity of earthly things,' he continued, 'and as led by Thy Holy Spirit seek first the kingdom of God and His righteousness, choosing rather to suffer affliction with the people of God than to enjoy the pleasures of sin.' In the pew in front of me, a young boy exchanged playful glances with a child nearby.

The Bethel chapel (Bethel meaning 'House of God' in Hebrew) is one of about 150 independent Gospel Standard Strict Baptist churches in Britain which hold fast to Calvinist theology. Members believe in the intrinsic evil of human nature and in 'predestination': that God has predetermined those who through His grace will believe and be saved, known as the elect. 'Strict' is a corruption of the word restricted: the unbaptised are not admitted to the Lord's Supper, or communion. Everything depends on the grace of God. When service times are published in church literature, they carry provisos such as 'God willing' and 'if the Lord will'. The Strict Baptists trace their origins to 1633 and the adoption of 'believers' baptism' (baptism through immersion as a teenager or adult) by a London group of Calvinistic separatists. They are not affiliated to the Baptist Union of Great Britain, the umbrella group for about 160,000 Baptists in this country, who have for the most part modified the strict Calvinism which characterised them in the eighteenth century and before. Dr Ian Hamnett of Bristol University, who has researched them, says they represent 'the most extreme form of High Calvinism extant in this, or possibly any, country'.

In Bedfordshire, the Strict Baptists were strongly influenced by John Bunyan, author of *The Pilgrim's Progress*. They believe today, as Bunyan did in the seventeenth century, that life is a perpetual battle between good and evil, a combat which in evangelical circles today goes by the name of 'spiritual warfare', and that salvation is the most important issue in life.

The congregation of nearly 200 included builders, businessmen, nurses and doctors. They were well dressed in sober but attractive clothes that seemed to speak of the Protestant work ethic and country life in early Victorian England. All the women wore ribboned hats; the older were in dark colours and the younger in long, flowing dresses. A baby was dressed in a Victorian-style lace bonnet.

There were many children and teenagers, who attend 'Sabbath school' in a classroom behind the church on Sunday afternoons.

Baptism in the church is still by total immersion, but at our service the baptistry was covered, and the focus of the church was the large, raised pulpit at the front. Bibles and hymn books awaited us in the pews and the service began quietly, as Mr Ramsbottom emerged from his vestry door and climbed into the pulpit.

John Watts, one of three deacons who announce the hymns at services, greet people at the door, visit the sick and do administrative work, announced a hymn, reading the first verse in full, and Mr Ramsbottom read thirty verses of St John's Gospel from the authorised King James version of the Bible, ending with: 'May God bless the reading of His word. May He help us in prayer.' Mr Ramsbottom's prayers were impromptu, and his delivery seemed influenced by an old biblical style, which he rendered in a Lancashire accent.

'Most holy and gracious Lord, we would come before Thee with reverence, realising something of Thy greatness and majesty and sovereignty and glory, and realising our own nothingness and sinfulness and guilt,' he said. 'Save us from everything which comes short. From all imitation and all hypocrisy. Oh to be real Christians, washed in the Redeemer's blood.' His sermon, which took up about half of the ninety-minute service, was in similar vein. He preached from the prophet Jeremiah who, he reminded us, is known as the weeping prophet. 'What would Jeremiah have said today?' he asked, bemoaning the breaking of 'God's holy law, God's sabbath, God's commandments' by a society that is 'turning our backs on God, forgetting his mercies'.

He described a 'craving, this longing for something bigger, better, greater'. He said: 'Never has our country had so much. Never has our country been so discontented.' His sermon was accompanied by heartfelt actions, raising his eyes heavenwards or casting them down where appropriate. 'We want our own way, our own thing,' he said. 'The whole human race by nature is blinded by sin and Satan to the glories of this fountain of living waters. Each one of us, we are ignorant of the truth. We are foolish as we are lost and ruined through sin. And we are spiritually blind.' After a blessing at the end, the congregation stood and chatted on the pavement.

I asked Suzanne Christian, aged seventeen and not long baptised, what the appeal was. 'They preach the Gospel,' she said simply, leaving me wondering about my ultimate destination.

SERVICES: Sundays, 10.30 a.m. and 6 p.m.; Thursdays, 7.30 p.m.; prayer meetings Monday, 7.30 p.m.

St Agnes Church
Easterside
MIDDLESBROUGH
Cleveland
(Tel: 01642 316144)

PRIEST-IN-CHARGE: The Rev. Jane Vaughan-Wilson.

ARCHITECTURE: Built in 1965. From the outside it resembles a spaceship, but suits an environment in which many feel alienated.

SERMON: Spirited lesson in parenting, love and forgiveness, based on the parable of the prodigal son.

MUSIC: Brisk organ playing, excellent acoustics and strong voices of the choir and congregation countered the forbidding environment.

LITURGY: Rite A in the Alternative Service Book seemed a sacred bastion of tradition in this modernist building.

AFTER-SERVICE CARE: Tea served sometimes. Coffee supplied in vicarage. Youngsters attend a junior church Sunday School during the service, and the church has started a joint youth project with the local branch library and community development teams.

SPIRITUAL HIGH: Incredible sensation of closeness to God.

St Agnes church is unmissable, but a passer-by on the main road that runs past the council estate where it is set might not know immediately what it is. The 100ft spire, a cross between a radio mast and a north-of-England version of the Eiffel Tower, dominates the landscape. Those who take the trouble to investigate and see the thin copper sheeting on the roof, the stark wooden cross outside and the exposed steel of the spire might imagine a religion as uncompromising as the landscape.

A challenging design, the church became for me a sign of resurrected hope in Middlesbrough's landscape of despair, where silent factories and neglected housing estates reflect the decline of Teesside's industrial base.

Inside, an embroidered wall-hanging celebrated a 'God of concrete, God of steel'. The dark purple ceiling was relieved only by a large roof light. The slate floor, pine benches and green synthetic fabric-covered kneelers, combined with strange pinkish lights hung from a green wooden frame suspended above the sanctuary, added to the sense of being a stranger in a strange land. The church was saved only by its altar, rough-hewn from limestone.

I was greeted warmly by two elderly men, but nearly everyone else, including the robed choir, was female. As we prepared to begin our worship, the 'vicar' emerged from the vestry to greet us, wearing a black shirt, clerical collar, white alb and green stole. The Rev. Jane Vaughan-Wilson was the first woman to be placed in charge of a parish in the York diocese, and was one of the first in the country to hold such a position.

She was at St Agnes before she could legally call herself priest. As a deacon in charge of a parish before the General Synod voted to ordain women priests, she could not celebrate communion or pronounce absolution after confession until she was ordained in the summer of 1994. Before her ordination as priest, she had to call in retired or neighbouring male clergy to celebrate communion.

On my visit, shortly before her ordination, Mrs Vaughan-Wilson opened with the announcement that the Rev. Chris Simmons, curate at nearby Kirkleatham, would celebrate communion that morning. Her husband, Colin, a primary school teacher, stood at the back of the church holding their baby, India, whom Mrs Vaughan-Wilson has been known to breast-feed in the vestry, an activity that compares with reports of a nearby clergyman who celebrates communion with his baby carried in a sling on his back.

Mrs Vaughan-Wilson's clear voice carried well and with authority, and the issue of her sex was soon forgotten as we progressed through the service. With her rosy cheeks, plump face and dark reddish hair, she seemed a living tribute to St Agnes herself, commemorated on a scarlet banner standing in one corner. St Agnes was condemned to burn at the stake in AD 304, when she spurned the amorous advances of the son of the Prefect of Rome. The flames were miraculously extinguished, but St Agnes was dispatched by sword.

Mrs Vaughan-Wilson preached her sermon from notes and began by recreating the parable of the prodigal son, bringing it forward 2,000 years and making it a story of a prodigal daughter. She said: 'I can talk about this because I am an elder sister. I was and still am a very good girl. When I was very little, somewhere along the line I realised something. I realised that if you are a good girl you get loved, or at least you get approved of. There is this fear when you are very little that there might not be enough love to go round. One way of securing myself some love was to earn it.' Referring to her own child, then aged one, she added: 'I find with India, now she is getting older, that it is very easy to show love when she is being good. It is much harder to know how to love her when she is being a nuisance and driving me up the wall. It is a challenge to me and all parents to somehow convey acceptance and love, but still to set boundaries and teach values.'

With high unemployment, regular break-ins and plagued by joyriders, the Easterside estate bears witness to the decline of the Teesside iron, steel and shipbuilding industries. Here, I felt as if God was speaking to me when I found my car still intact outside the church as I left. And at the sign of the peace, when many congregations exchange 'air kisses' or perfunctory handshakes, the congregation of about forty sprang into energetic life. The peace took longer than usual, because everyone was determined to hug, shake hands vigorously or exchange quick gossip with everyone else in a display of warmth. After the collection, Mr Simmons took over to celebrate communion.

As the male voice sounded out, a slight tremor seemed to go through the many elderly women in the congregation, who seemed proud and protective of Mrs Vaughan-Wilson as woman deacon. Mr Simmons led us through the eucharistic liturgy with inspiration, bringing it to life in a way that few can do. But, as a man, he nevertheless seemed out of place.

Something of the sorrow of the women denied the priestly ministry for so long came to me as, kneeling for the eucharistic prayer from my seat in the south aisle, all I could see of Mrs Vaughan-Wilson was her hair, bound with a blue ribbon in a ponytail, drooping sadly over her bowed head behind the altar. The last of our five hymns, 'Praise to the holiest in the height', by John Henry Newman, the founder of the Oxford Movement, seemed then an ironic acknowledgement to the enduring patriarchy in the Church of England.

SUNDAY SERVICES: Sung eucharist 10.30 a.m.; evening service 6.30 p.m. on last Sunday of the month.

The King's Church
Bryn Coch School
Victoria Road
MOLD
Clwyd
(Tel: 01352 757477)

PASTOR: Idris Williams.

ARCHITECTURE: School hall with the use of some classrooms for creche and young church (3–13) classes.

SERMON: Passionate hour-long discourse on humanity's thirst for truth, and the inclination in some to quench that thirst with sin.

MUSIC: Lively five-piece band played modern hymns and catchy gospel songs.

LITURGY: Order of Service structured around praise and worship at the beginning and prayers at the end.

AFTER-SERVICE CARE: Pastoral follow-up, with prayer and Bible study groups meeting during the week.

SPIRITUAL HIGH: A party atmosphere.

The King's Church when I visited met in a low building in a bleak Mold shopping centre, an earthly embodiment of the kind of afterlife to which conservatives like myself hope some modern architects might be condemned for eternity. It now meets in a school hall nearby.

The church is one of a growing number of evangelical 'new churches', or non-denominational Christian groupings which seem to thrive under the leadership of one or more charismatic individuals. It was founded several years ago in Newport, Gwent, by Pastor Ray Bevan, and has links with similar churches worldwide. Pastor Idris Williams, a former television scriptwriter, left Newport to start or, as evangelicals term it, to 'plant' a sister church in Mold, and numbers at the two-and-a-half-hour evening service have grown from a handful of founder members to more than 200. A leaflet handed to all newcomers is unequivocal: 'Our beliefs are fundamental and evangelical, our sole text book being the Bible.' It affirms belief in the Virgin Birth, the miracles, the bodily resurrection, the ascension and the Second Coming of Christ.

The church is charismatic, and members often practise the 'gifts of the spirit' such as speaking in tongues, interpretation of the tongues and prophecy.

Mr Williams, who used to write stand-up comedy sketches for entertainers and has performed in variety acts in Wales, is using his showbusiness skills to good effect in Mold. A well-rehearsed band, with drums, electric guitars and female singers, was warming up as we arrived, their sound relayed to us through enormous speakers. Members of the congregation sprang into life at the opening beat of the first hymn, standing with arms and hands raised high, many clapping, jigging and swaying to the music. We went through a series of popular modern church songs, including 'Blessed be the name of the Lord', when the congregation performed a ritual Bucks Fizz-style dance routine as the heat built up inside the yellow walls. Mr Williams explained afterwards: 'Dancing is scriptural. David danced before the ark, and in the Psalms people danced in praise of the Lord.' Mr Williams interjected frequently with words of prayer and inspiration.

'The Holy Spirit will be moving now among people's lives, changing people, setting people free,' he said. After forty minutes of singing, Mr Williams launched into his sermon. People were thirsting for the truth, he said.

'They look for different things to quench that thirst. There are people living on pornography, in sexual immorality, living on drugs, living on alcohol. I am not condemning them but it is drowning them. They want Jesus.' The rich too were thirsty, he added. The thirst of all these people 'has not come from God, it has come from Satan'.

After his sermon, he invited those in need of prayer to the front and about twenty people walked up. He addressed a woman. 'That darkness is going,' he said. 'From now on, my sister, you will be dancing in your soul. Receive it now.' By now one woman was sobbing, while another at the back, arms raised, cried: 'Receive, receive, oh receive.' Thirsting only for strength to complete the 200-plus mile drive south, I went alone into the wild darkness of north Wales.

SUNDAY SERVICES: 10.30 a.m. and 6.30 p.m. weekly.

Gedling Baptist Church
Grey Goose Inn
Arnold Lane
Gedling
NOTTINGHAM
NG2 4DA
(Tel: 01602 691290)

MINISTER: The Rev. Graham Coventry.

PUBLICAN: Frank Starbuck.

ARCHITECTURE: Mock Georgian, built 1950s.

SERMON: Christian teaching, based on a trick with a 'magic box', that eternal life has more to do with knowing God than with going to church.

MUSIC: Rock guitarist played popular hymns from *Songs of Fellowship*, with words projected on to a screen.

LITURGY: Underlying liturgy of 'the word', Bible reading, preaching, confession, praise, worship and prayer.

AFTER-SERVICE CARE: Invitation to a local home for tea or coffee. Monday night housegroup, discussion groups and offer of a follow-up visit at home.

SPIRITUAL HIGH: Pub-like feeling of warmth and friendship induced by a different kind of spirit.

Not wanting to be spotted entering a pub at 10.30 on a Sunday morning, I parked my car round the back of the Grey Goose Inn in Gedling, Nottingham, and almost ran through the side entrance. I need not have worried. The bar was closed and the drinkers were probably in bed, sleeping off the results of the rock party the night before. There was only a cleaner, and two people washing glasses and tidying up behind the bar.

Since March 1993, a group of Nottingham Baptists, determined to take church to the people rather than expect them to come to it, have met in the Ganders music bar of the Grey Goose for forty-five minutes of worship, praise and prayer.

Opposite the site of the Gedling Colliery, which closed in 1991, and between a private and a council housing estate, the pub seemed an ideal venue for the Baptists' new church because it is at the heart of the community. A vivid green poster outside states: 'No strings attached. No hidden clauses. Jesus loves you. Just as you are.'

We sat on low, cushioned bar stools; a Chesterfield sofa served as the front 'pew'. Two sisters, Jodie, four, and Jessica, five, perched on high bar stools at the back. Beneath the darkened disco lights, the minister, the Rev. Graham Coventry, stood with his microphone on the disco floor, ready to lead us in the service.

Most of the twenty adults were in their Sunday best, with their many children also smartly dressed in party clothes. Most said they would visit a pub occasionally, but were not regular drinkers.

Baptists are traditionally evangelical Christians and are renowned for their missionary zeal. The Gedling Baptists are no exception. Mr Coventry visits the pub regularly during opening hours, although he sticks to Coke, and had recently braved a bikers' night to talk and answer questions. Most of the church members are adult converts, having had little or no contact with churches in their youth. He runs discussion groups called 'you must be joking' groups, that being the most common response from people invited for the first time.

Much of the worship was spontaneous, and the structure is fluid and can change each week. Mr Coventry began:

We are just going to bow our heads for a word of prayer first and ask the Lord Jesus to be with us in a special way. Father, we thank you this lovely Sunday morning. The sunshine so often reminds us of how warm and great you are. We thank you that as well as the sunshine outside, there is the joy of knowing you on the inside.

I need some help now because I want to declare that Jesus is alive. There are people who live around here and do not know that Jesus is alive.

Simon Nicholas, a rock guitarist, played, and his wife Ann helped us with 'actions' to the first hymn; these involved shouting and waving our hands.

The Bible readings consisted of two verses, from St John's Gospel and the prophet Jeremiah, and the sermon was aimed primarily at the children. Mr Coventry said: 'I was thinking about friendship with God this week. Real life is being friends with Jesus, being friends with God.' Matthew Scott, six, held up a tissue-paper sign: 'Meet and know them.' Two other children held up other signs, and Mr Coventry proceeded to crumple up the tissues and put them into a 'magic box'. The tissues seemed to disappear, to the silent fascination of the children, while he pulled out another, 'Be friends with God', muttering that he hoped nobody would be too worried about the theology of this trick. The children were then sent to the back, where they sat on the floor filling in worksheets on 'being friends with God', while we were encouraged to give thanks for 'the good things that God has done', to pray for the community and 'to listen' to God in a few moments of silence. Some members prayed out loud, before we moved into a session of praise, led by Mr Nicholas.

Afterwards, some of the members explained the appeal. Lynn Walton, a community care assistant with three children, said: 'I think it is great. We need to be where people are. Most people won't come to a church.' Brian Matthews, former miner and now a part-time postman, said: 'It feels like a church to me, not like a pub.' Mr Coventry said: 'Jesus is far better than any opiate this world can offer, whether it is drink, drugs or anything else. It is much more exciting to be a Christian than it is to imbibe any of those kinds of stimuli.' He referred me to the Acts of the Apostles 2. Here, St Peter and the disciples were accused of drunkenness after speaking in tongues on the day of Pentecost in Jerusalem. Addressing the crowd, Peter defended his apostles, stating they could not possibly be drunk, because it was only nine o'clock in the morning.

SUNDAY SERVICE: 10.30 a.m.

Taizé evening
All Saints Church
Gobowen
OSWESTRY
SY11 3LL
(Tel: 01691 655469/662125)

VICAR: The Rev. Michael Withey.
ARCHITECTURE: Built this century in Early English style, the church was recently devastated by fire and restored with bare whitewashed walls, polished stone and pews arranged diagonally. Wonderful feel of sacramental simplicity.
SERMON: The vicar, in a brief talk at the beginning, explained the significance of the act of worship to come.
LITURGY: Prayers drawn up by the vicar, set around the music.
MUSIC: Beautiful, restorative chants from the Taizé community in France, best heard unaccompanied but here sung with piano and electric organ.
AFTER-SERVICE CARE: Tea, coffee and cakes with entertaining chat, plus a bookstall run by Mold Christian Bookshop with a wide range of Taizé books and other Christian products.
SPIRITUAL HIGH: Extraordinarily calm, restful, meditative.

Outside, pale yellow daffodils shone in the frosted grass under a full moon, creating an unearthly atmosphere appropriate to this unusual service in a small town on the borders of England and Wales. At All Saints in Gobowen a banner at the back of the church stated: 'The Earth Is The Lord's', hinting at an underlying theology more ancient than the Christ-centred liturgy. Inside, the pale, polished stone glowed in the light of dozens of candles arranged in the shape of a cross through the chancel and ascending to the altar.

Soft, starry and vaguely familiar music played through a concealed sound system as the golden pine pews filled with people of all ages, many brought there by coach. We sat in absolute silence while the white-robed priest, Michael Withey, and his assistants, in similar attire, prepared for the service. One, the Rev. Anne Stratford, then a non-stipendiary deacon in a neighbouring parish, was herself later ordained priest at Lichfield Cathedral.

The mystical, peaceful atmosphere was familiar to all who have visited the Taizé community, founded by Roger Schutz-Marsauche, now known as Brother Roger, fifty years ago in Burgundy, France. The aim of the community, which consists of 'brothers' from all Christian denominations, is reconciliation between all people. It has become a centre of pilgrimage for thousands of Christians, in particular the young.

The Taizé style of worship involves melodic, repetitive chanting combined with silence and simple, evocative prayers. It is gradually being taken up by churches throughout Britain, who use its forms for occasional acts of worship. As we began, Mr Withey explained: 'Taizé is a place of encouragement, hope and strength. It is not just pretty lights, tinkly music, prayer, stillness and peace . . . It is about an encounter with the living God who never wants to send us away in the same way that we come.' Such services were not for relaxation but were 'a powerhouse to energise us where we can go out and face life with the power of the risen Christ'.

The clergy lit lamps as we began. Many of the chants were in Latin. They remained in my head for weeks after the service. We progressed through the liturgy, the clergy in turn reciting the words on the printed sheets we had been handed at the door, while we responded accordingly. One prayer was surprisingly 'inclusive', or non-sexist, ascribing a female personality to God.

During intercessionary prayers, to which we sang a haunting refrain, Mr Withey pleaded: 'Lord Jesus Christ, light of the world, enable us to discern your presence in every human being.' He ended: 'How important it is that love should bring openness and that we should be able to speak truly to one another.' Mr Withey and Mrs Stratford walked down the aisle, lighting the individual candles on our pews, which we then held and took to the altar, forming a circle as we prayed and sang together before departing into the damp mist.

Over coffee, the elderly gentleman behind me turned out to have been the Right Rev. John Davies, Bishop of Shrewsbury, in mufti. As we tucked into *bara brith*, a form of Welsh fruit cake, a number of other collarless men confessed to me with a faint air of embarrassment that they also were clergy in disguise. Whether they were secretly picking up tips to take back to their own churches remained unclear.

SERVICES: telephone for details.

***The Joy Mass, then at St Mary and St John Oxford
and now at St Clement's, Marston Road
OXFORD
(Tel: 01865 248735)***

RECTOR: The Rev. Bruce Gillingham.

ARCHITECTURE: Early Victorian, influenced by Norman and Georgian architecture.

SERMON: Brief exposition on why Christ told a rich man to give money to the poor, and the need for self-sacrifice.

LITURGY: Adaptation of modern Anglican prayer book, with essential elements only retained.

MUSIC: Imaginative and loud religious rock, played well and enthusiastically by youngsters from a local rock band.

AFTER-SERVICE CARE: Newcomers welcome to join prayers at the end.

SPIRITUAL HIGH: At once high and low.

The sound of the rock band Talking Heads' hit 'Road to Nowhere' was not the music I would expect to emanate from a traditional Anglican parish church. Inside the church, the contrast between expectation and reality increased, with white cloths hung over the intricate stone decoration, the backdrop for a local band, The Unlucky Millionth, comprising guitarists, drummer and a woman vocalist, who played modern startling settings to ancient liturgies. The church was in almost total darkness, dimly lit by candles. The faces of the young men and women moving slowly to the music, were hidden in shadows. The cloth screen showed video footage of a fat man exploding in gluttony, from the Monty Python film *The Meaning of Life*.

I had arrived at the rehearsal for the monthly 'Joy' service at Cowley St John, Oxford, where it was held until the vicar there, the Rev. Martin Flatman, decided to convert to Roman Catholicism. The Joy service has now moved to St Clement's, Oxford.

Aged thirty-three at the time, I was one of the oldest people there. Joy might offend the sensibilities of some, but the dozens of teenagers and young people, many waif-like, slim and ethereal in the latest grunge fashions, looked the sort who under any other circumstance would not be seen dead inside a church. The service is an attempt to communicate the Christian message to young people in the language of youth. Father Flatman, an Anglo-Catholic who says the Church of England does not have the authority to ordain women priests, was an unusual traditionalist in that he was a charismatic Anglo-Catholic, believing that speaking in tongues, healing and prophecy can all be part of the ministry.

Joy, begun in 1990 by the Oxford Youth Works (a Christian organisation) is run by the congregation. It is held at Cowley St John by invitation, and a diffident seventeen-year-old known as Mossy was leader for our service. Under church law, only a priest can celebrate communion, hence the presence of Fr Flatman at Joy. But it was evident that this was a pleasure and not a chore for this effervescent priest. Wearing a vivid cerise chasuble, unable or unwilling to remove a dimpled grin from his rosy-cheeked face, he tapped his feet and jogged to the music at the back of the church until needed for the brief celebration at the front.

The rehearsal over, there were a few moments of meditation. On one of the coldest days of the year, the effect of the overhead electric heaters was barely noticeable. But the chill quickly disappeared as we then stood and bopped to the opening number, Donna Summer's 'State of Independence'. 'It's like an acid house party. You normally have to pay to get into something like this,' one amazed newcomer said. In fact, it was not the least like an acid house party. The atmosphere of contentment and enjoyment was induced by faith and spirituality, not by drugs.

Joy uses the modern liturgy of the Alternative Service Book rewritten in places. It works fairly well, although anyone who did not know the service book well might not have recognised it. Parts were heavily adapted and set to rock music. There were no hymns but we sang pop songs, with the words projected on to the screen. We sang along with the band, as if taking part in a form of religious group karaoke. At one point, band members acted out a parable on the pursuit of wealth, in silhouette, from behind the screen. We watched the video of the fat man explode, a lesson in the deadly sin of gluttony. Words projected on to the screen asked us: 'How much do you need to be happy?' and gave us Rockefeller's answer: 'A little bit more.'

All this took place between and around the Old Testament and Gospel readings, followed by a sermon based on the story of the rich man as told by St Mark. This man was told by Christ to sell everything he had and give to the poor, enticed by the promise of riches in heaven. Jim Barker, aged twenty-five, took this as his text, not preaching at us but speaking about himself. 'As a rich young man, I ask myself what trip was this man on,' he said. 'He obeyed the commandments. He lived a righteous life. He went to the synagogue; like I also come to church. I do good works; I work for Oxfam. God, what a saint I am. But that obviously was not the point, and Jesus knew this. He had another agenda.'

He described the 'retail therapy' of the 1980s, the acquisition of material possessions, 'where we pay others to feel good'. A picture of the Queen was projected on to the screen. The Christian alternative was not to walk around in sackcloth and ashes, filled with self-hatred, Jim told us. 'Jesus teaches us something more than that. The way of being without riches, of giving to the poor, is sacrifice through embracing that which we do not know.'

The intercessionary prayers before communion were moving testimonies to the conflicts experienced by the young. 'Dear Lord, show us what to spend money on and what not to spend money on,' said one teenager, barely out of boyhood. 'Do we really need an expensive stereo or flash car? Or do we really need love?' A girl pleaded: 'Help us to give what we have to others, our possessions and our love.'

After communion and the blessing, the congregation broke up into groups to chat or dance a little longer. Some went to a side chapel for prayers. There had been no collection; offerings could be put in a plate at the back. Fr Flatman blessed us as we left. I took one last look at the intricate stone tracery, the darkness and candlelight; the mystery of why a modern audio system and thumping music did not seem out of place in this sanctified place. Words projected on to the screen advised: 'The best place to hide from God is in the church, among all the paraphernalia of religion. There's a good chance that he'll never find you there.'

Some adults visiting Joy have said it makes them feel far from God. Perhaps they should ask themselves who has moved.

SUNDAY SERVICES: Joy mass takes place on the last Sunday of the month at 9 p.m.

Trinity College
Broad St
OXFORD
OX1 3BH
(Tel: 01865 279886)

CHAPLAIN FELLOW: The Rev. Trevor Williams.

ARCHITECTURE: The modest exterior makes doubly astonishing the masterpiece of English baroque inside. The college sought the advice of Sir Christopher Wren for what became the first chapel in Oxford to be designed on pure classical principles, built between 1691 and 1694.

SERMON: Professor Leslie Houlden, of King's College London, preached on Austin Farrer, a chaplain fellow of Trinity 1935–60, in whose name a fund was being created.

MUSIC: Organ scholar Thomas Kell and assistant Sarah Rawling directed a mixed choir through sung Holy Communion.

LITURGY: The modern Rite A for Holy Communion from the Alternative Service Book, with some authorised improvements.

AFTER-SERVICE CARE: Orange juice or sherry, and an invitation to dine.

SPIRITUAL HIGH: Calming to take communion in such surroundings.

To enter the dark, carved, baroque interior of the Chapel, Trinity College, described as 'one of the most perfect ensembles of the late seventeenth century in the whole country' by Pevsner's architectural guide, is to encounter a world at the same time ancient and modern. The chapel celebrated the 300th anniversary of its consecration in 1994.

Before we began, Sue Williams, the chaplain's wife, lit the candles that run along the pews and which are still used as the main source of light. As we stood among the shadows in the deep oak stalls on each side of the chapel, the carvings, thought to be by Grinling Gibbons, seemed to take on a life of their own in the flickering candlelight amid the descending darkness. The lustrous effect created by the combination of carved walnut, pear, lime and *Juniperus bermudiana*, the latter described by one early traveller as 'sweet like Cedar', beneath a magnificent painting of the Ascension by Berchet, helped evoke an obscure longing for ancient catholic and academic tradition.

Outside, statues on the tower representing Geometry, Astronomy, Theology and Medicine stood guard over a scene of relaxed informality. And worship here also included some surprising challenges to tradition.

The well-schooled choir was not the usual one of boys and men, but mixed male and female voices, including a woman deacon, the Rev. Sue Irwin, from Kidlington, later to be ordained. The chaplain fellow, Trevor Williams, narrowly defeated an opponent of women priests to represent the university's Anglican clergy on the General Synod. Mr Williams is one of two remaining chaplains who have part of their salaries paid out of the Common University Fund. As an elected fellow of Trinity, he is a full member of the governing body and also tutors in theology, specialising in doctrine.

Coincident with the tercentenary of the chapel's consecration, the governing body created a fund in the name of Austin Farrer, a distinguished priest and theologian who was chaplain of Trinity from 1935 to 1960. The preacher at our service was Leslie Houlden, who succeeded Farrer as chaplain in 1960, is now Professor of Theology at King's College, London, and recently edited a book of Farrer's sermons. Mr Williams succeeded Professor Houlden in 1970.

He began by announcing details of the Farrer Appeal. 'His writings include works of a great theological and philosophical significance and also of a profound spirituality,' he said.

The chaplain continued: 'I would like to invite all to come and receive communion who can do so with sincerity, with some sense of its meaning. Some of you may prefer not to, in which case you are invited to come to the altar for a blessing or stay seated.' Professor Houlden, in his sermon, said: 'Farrer was a many-sided genius but oddly difficult to place. Everybody admits his brilliance, but you search indexes in vain for references to his work. And this was true whether you think of his philosophical writings or of his dazzling but strange books on the Gospel of Mark and the Revelation of John.' Farrer made his name by his sermons, he said. 'Preaching was for Farrer no light task. It was not a mere adjunct to the business of writing academic books. He took very seriously the charge of pastor.' Sung eucharist in the evening is a rare treat in most Oxford colleges, evensong being more common. The congregation, mainly undergraduates and postgraduates, included a handful of Roman Catholics, such as Paul Rozario, an undergraduate from Singapore reading law, who is chapel secretary, and Daniel Seward, an undergraduate reading philosophy and theology, who led the intercessionary prayers. Most wore gowns, a mixture of the full-length scholar's gown and the abbreviated commoner's variety. At the west end sat the college president, Sir John Burgh, former director of the British Council, with his wife Ann.

Professor Houlden sat in the equivalent stall across the aisle. The chapel, which seats 120, felt intimate, and seemed well-filled by the choir of about sixteen and the congregation, of a similar size.

The college was founded by Sir Thomas Pope in 1555 but our service marked the beginning of the 300th anniversary celebrations of the consecration of the present chapel, rebuilt under Ralph Bathurst, president of Trinity from 1664 to 1704.

In our intercessions, Mr Seward led us in prayer for the Queen, and for all victims of war, especially in Bosnia, Somalia and Northern Ireland. 'May God protect them from men's arrogance and crime, and bring them peace and justice,' he said.

He prayed that 'we may receive the grace to follow Christ in resisting temptation', leaving at the end a few seconds of silence to 'pray for our own private intentions'. The 'peace' was refreshingly old-fashioned, and in the preparation of the bread and wine Mr Williams used blessings offered as an alternative to those in the Alternative Service Book. Over the bread he said: 'Blessed are you Lord God of all creation. Through your goodness we have this bread to offer . . . it will become for us the bread of life.' The wine, in a pre-Reformation silver gilt chalice, was 'fruit of the vine and work of human hands. It will become our spiritual drink.' As the light finally faded outside, the candles flickered more brightly, lightening our darkness as we headed home.

SUNDAY SERVICES: term time only: Holy Communion 9 a.m.; evenson 6 p.m. (sung eucharist once a term).

St Nicholas Church
HMS Drake
HM Naval Base Devonport
PLYMOUTH
Devon
PL2 2BG
(Tel: 01752 555266)

CHAPLAIN: The Rev. Simon Golding, RN.

ARCHITECTURE: Completed 1907, resembles a large upturned tub on the verge of sliding into the sea.

SERMON: The Rev. Paul Martin, RN, preached staunchly on the responsibility Christians have to share their faith.

MUSIC: Small choir of three women and one man sang astonishingly loudly, adding a harmonious top line to the deep-timbred voices of the veterans.

LITURGY: Anglican rite enlivened by poetic additions from the officiant, the Rev. Ned Kelly, RN.

AFTER-SERVICE CARE: Entertaining tales of the high seas from veteran navy hands.

SPIRITUAL HIGH: Ups and downs throughout the service, with interjections from seagulls adding a sense of romance.

For a shameless landlubber who feels seasick at the sight of a cross-Channel ferry, the opportunity to attend a Royal Navy chaplaincy service on dry land, at the 300-year-old Devonport naval base in Plymouth, could not be missed. We were met at the gate by two navy gunners, who seemed confused over whether to deflect journalists or welcome churchgoers.

The secure fencing that protects the base from unwelcome visitors also protects the nineteenth-century building from vandalism, and from the outside it appears in pristine condition. Inside, the white walls are lined with memorial plaques commemorating men killed in action, and ships' emblems decorate the pillars. Over our heads was suspended a large model of the Elizabethan flagship the *Golden Hind*, the 100-ton ship sailed by Sir Francis Drake to South America in 1578.

The church is dedicated to St Nicholas, the patron saint of sailors, captives, children and Russia, and the saint who has been mythologised as Santa Claus. The service was taken by the Rev. Ned Kelly, RN, and his assistant, Capt Philip Slater, of the Church Army, read the Gospel.

The Royal Navy has its own Archdeaconry headed by the Chaplain of the Fleet, the Ven. Michael Bucks. All Royal Navy chaplains hold the Queen's commission as chaplains and are licensed by the Archbishop of Canterbury. The Archbishop delegates much of the day-to-day responsibility for Anglican chaplaincy in the Armed Forces to the Bishop to the Forces, the Right Rev. John Kirkham, Bishop of Sherborne.

As we began, the commander of HMS *Drake*, Lieutenant Commander Jamie Bardolf-Smith, and his family sat in the front pew. Captain Mike Thomas, the captain of HMS *Drake*, sat behind him, with the veterans behind them both.

Some, chiefly those with the thickest beards and most weathered faces, had tears in their eyes as the organ struck up and we launched into 'Fight the good fight with all thy might!' The organist, Roy Wilkins, and a handful of civilians in the congregation had come in from the local community, after gaining entry with a pass issued after a security check to anyone who wishes to become a regular church member.

We progressed through the Rite A communion service from the Alternative Service Book of the Church of England. The highlight came at the end, when the veterans, in deep, strong voices which echoed around the wooden collar-beam truss roof, said the Naval Prayer, first included in the Prayer Book in 1662, and sang the last verse of 'Eternal Father, strong to save'.

HMS *Drake* is a 'concrete frigate', a shore establishment and base for all frigates, Types 23, 22 and 21, where sailors are put up when their ship comes in for a refit.

A few ships were alongside during our visit but, apart from a small party there for a baptism, there were few serving sailors at our service. The church, a barn-like structure which can seat 440, was half filled instead by veterans from the HMS *Rodney* and HMS *Vanguard* associations, enjoying their annual reunions at the base. Frank Curran, of HMS *Vanguard*, said: 'Most of us did go to church on the battleship. It was not compulsory, but we were God-fearing boys in those days.' God-fearing maybe, but with a bearing that suggested a frightening fearlessness were action to beckon again.

SUNDAY SERVICES: Holy Communion 8.30 a.m.; the eucharist 10.30 a.m.

The Parish Church of St Mary the Virgin
Church Square
RYE
East Sussex
TN31 7HH
(Tel: 01797 222430)

TEAM RECTOR: The Rev. Martin Sheppard.

ARCHITECTURE: Cruciform structure built in twelfth century, reduced to a ruin by French invaders in 1377 and rebuilt by 1500. The tower has the second oldest clock (1562) in England.

SERMON: Skilful analysis of Gospel reading in just under five minutes by the Rev. Paddy Buxton, who was rector when I visited.

LITURGY: Perfect setting for language of the Prayer Book.

AFTER-SERVICE CARE: None, because rector must dash to nearby church for 9.15 a.m. service at Rye harbour. Hoped-for invitation to a rubber of bridge not forthcoming.

SPIRITUAL HIGH: Serene start to the day.

Walking through the deserted cobbled streets of Rye for 8 o'clock communion at St Mary's, it was difficult not to feel that every step was being observed by the devious Miss Elizabeth Mapp of Tilling, the place name given to the Sussex town by the novelist E.F. Benson, one-time mayor of Rye and son of Archbishop Benson.

Passing by lace-curtained windows up the hill dominated by the stone and flint church, I felt Miss Mapp would have smirked that the 8 o'clock communion is popular with many Anglicans because in most churches it lasts only half an hour, has no hymns, no sermon, and allows them to take their weekly sacrament while leaving the rest of the day free for secular entertainments doubly enjoyable after righteous attendance at church when most are still in bed.

At St Mary's, however, I was surprised to find that the congregation has requested a weekly sermon from the vicar, an indication perhaps that the town still merits its ancient reputation as a model puritan community.

Women outnumbered the men at the service, as is normal in many Anglican parish churches. Most were retired, or the wives of retired professionals, or descended from the smugglers, fishermen and shopkeepers who have populated the town for 900 years. They sat one or two to a pew, numbers down on the usual thirty, with only the stalwarts fit enough to venture out so early after their exertions at the parish barn dance the night before. Judy Brown, a doctor's wife, who stood out in the front pew as particularly bright-eyed, is a former Kent golf champion, and was due on the links at 9 a.m.

The then rector, the Rev. Paddy Buxton, was a late ordinand and a former group chairman of Duracell Europe. His management skills found a fruitful outlet in balancing the needs of the different congregations at St Mary's.

Differences over matters such as the positioning of the altar were put to the vote. The congregation at the main service, which averages 100 people, and uses the modern liturgy from the Anglican Alternative Service Book, voted three to one for a mobile altar to be moved into the crossing between the nave and chancel. The more traditionalist 8 o'clock congregation, which has opted for the 1662 Book of Common Prayer, voted three to one that communion should be celebrated and taken at the high altar in the sanctuary beyond the chancel.

St Mary's is known locally as 'the cathedral on the marsh' because of its size. The high altar is 20 yards from the nave and, although Mr Buxton used a microphone, he and his assistant, Edwin Gibson, a church warden, seemed mere specks, the rector's voice a disembodied echo from afar.

The service began with announcements and proceeded through a shortened version of the communion service in the Prayer Book, a liturgy that seemed luxuriantly at home in this twelfth-century structure, used to store gunpowder to be used against the Armada during the reign of Elizabeth I. 'Put on the whole armour of God,' we heard from the epistle to the Ephesians. 'For we wrestle not against flesh and blood, but against principalities, against powers, against the rulers of the darkness of this world.' After the Gospel and the Creed, there was silence as the congregation awaited the sermon. Mr Buxton began his long journey from the altar to the pulpit at the end of the nave. His footsteps echoed around the church as he progressed on his brisk but seemingly endless walk through the chancel, choir and crossing. Mr Buxton, a 'catholic evangelical' who supports women priests, a rarity in the Chichester diocese, preached on St John's description of Christ's healing of the nobleman's son at Capernaum.

With only ten minutes to go before the end of the service,

Mr Buxton disappeared back into the distance for the confession. 'We acknowledge and bewail our manifold sins and wickedness, Which we, from time to time, most grievously have committed,' we said, heads bowed and kneeling humbly. 'The remembrance of them is grievous unto us; the burden of them is intolerable.' Never did an absolution seem more effective than after such a confession as this, or the ensuing communion feel more complete after such an absolution.

SUNDAY SERVICES: communion 8 a.m.; parish communion 10.30 a.m.; evensong 6 p.m.

The Waterfront Church
Forte Posthouse Hotel
Herbert Walker Avenue,
SOUTHAMPTON
(Tel: 01703 672277)

PASTOR: The Rev. Trevor Waldock.

ARCHITECTURE: Postmodernist style, which suited a postmodernist church in a hotel.

SERMON: The congregation was transfixed by an eloquent talk from the athlete Kriss Akabusi, whose winning ingredients were the willingness to laugh at himself and an astonishing turn of speed as he raced through his complex and gripping life story.

LITURGY: A 'play' in which a marital tragedy was enacted on stage. The moral message seemed to be that we should examine the beams in our own eyes before attacking the motes in our partners'.

MUSIC: Three Christian 'numbers' from a duet, Peter Emberley and Sharron Pearcy.

AFTER-SERVICE CARE: Coffee and a host of counsellors and helpers ready to answer any questions.

SPIRITUAL HIGH: Exhilarating and, like a race, faintly exhausting.

The athlete Kriss Akabusi, looking racy in a light green shirt and brown trousers, warned us that the last time he spoke in public a member of the audience threw a missile at him because he went on for so long. 'I like to talk,' he explained, grinning.

We were in the unlikely setting of the Novotel Southampton, a modern hotel, where the Waterfront Church was founded to counter a conviction that church was 'boring, irrelevant and hostile', and to confront attempts to debunk historical Christianity. The church has since moved to the Forte Posthouse.

The ambience was somewhat like that of a business conference, complete with questionnaires on the chairs and plastic pens with which to fill them out. We were invited to write down the question we would most like to ask a creator-God, assuming he existed and we were granted five minutes in his presence. 'Typically, the Waterfront Church guarantees people a safe place to come and hear a timeless message in a culturally relevant way that respects people's anonymity, desire for space and time to think things through,' said pastor Trevor Waldock.

Earlier, I had asked Akabusi what question he was asked most often. The surprising answer was: 'Did you enjoy the *Big Breakfast*?' Channel 4's weekday morning show, on which he had been a guest presenter.

At the Novotel church every chair was taken in the carpeted conference room. There were large numbers of teenagers in baggy sweatshirts, jeans and Doc Martens. A few adults were squeezed between them. Akabusi's wife Monika and his daughters, Ashanti, aged nine, and Shakira, six, sat in the front row. Normally, two large children's groups run in parallel with the adults' service.

The service opened with a song, 'Living Hope', from Pete Emberley and Sharron Pearcy, who sang and strummed guitars. Then the leader, Trevor Waldock, explained the beginnings of the church formed 'with the specific aim that it would be a church for people who did not want to go to church', based on the idea of 'putting Jesus in the context of the 1990s'.

After watching a morality play, we were introduced to the main performance, from Akabusi, who has retired from athletics and taken up Bible studies, public speaking and addressing schoolchildren. Working through the charity Christians in Sport, he preaches at different churches and receives enough invitations to keep him busy.

'Do you have dreams?' he asked us. 'I have had many, and sometimes the dreams have come true. For me, one of the biggest dreams in my life was that I would go to the Olympic Games, stand on the awards rostrum and then go "Yaaaaah!"' He yelled this so loud that we jumped.

He then described (using hands and feet) leaving the starting block in the final of the Barcelona Olympic 400-metre hurdles in 1992: 'A big brown shape comes past me. This is not what I call a dream; this is a nightmare.' The race was won by the American Kevin Young, although Akabusi set a new British record. 'There I was in third place and yet still the fastest man in British history. There I was a failure. I had not made it. I was not the best.' Then he grinned, and pulled his bronze medal from his pocket, and the congregation cheered. He said he had realised, on the rostrum, that he had nevertheless done his best. 'Now when I look at this baby in my pocket, I realise I am a champion,' he said.

He described growing up in poverty dreaming of a 'lovely car, lovely family, nice threads'. When he obtained his dream car, a

At a Service Near You

Mercedes, he wanted a bigger, better one. The turning point came after the Commonwealth Games in Edinburgh in 1986, while reading a Good News Bible in his hotel room. 'There was a guy in there. Obviously I had used his name before, but I never realised he actually lived. I thought he was like the tooth fairy and Father Christmas.' The following spring, while training in California, he begged Jesus to 'let me know if you are really who you say you are'.

Akabusi grinned again and said: 'That was the biggest or best mistake I ever made. That night I went to bed and I had what I call a vision.' He heard a verse from Matthew's Gospel. 'I shouted "Jesus!" Then I looked around because it is not cool to shout Jesus in the middle of the night. I got out my Filofax and wrote it down. In the morning there it was, my baptism by the Holy Spirit at 0300 hours. So I went down to the track. There they all were, Roger Black, Daley Thompson, the guys. I said: "Guys, guys, I met Jesus last night." They said: "Are you crazy?"' Christianity has worked for Akabusi. He now has the bigger Mercedes, with the number plate ECC 724, his favourite chapter and verse from Ecclesiastes. But even without the trappings of material success, he would still be a powerful advocate of a faith that works, because of the joy and courage it has given to him.

SUNDAY SERVICE: 8–9 p.m.

St Etheldreda's
West Quantoxhead
near WATCHET
Somerset
(Tel: 01278 741501)

RECTOR (of the seven parishes in the Quantoxhead group): The Rev. Andrew Stevens.

ARCHITECTURE: Built by the architect John Norton for £16,000 in 1854–56 of Doulting stone from Shepton Mallet, with solid English oak roof.

SERMON: Preached from notes, based closely on biblical texts in traditional evangelical style.

MUSIC: Amateur choir, (sometimes accompanied by one of the few playable barrel organs in the southwest) gives cheerful lead to enthusiastic congregation.

LITURGY: Standard Anglican rite.

AFTER-SERVICE CARE: Tea, coffee and biscuits and local gossip beneath the Somerset sun.

SPIRITUAL HIGH: Intimate and friendly atmosphere, with an open-hearted welcome for all.

I parked in blazing sunshine in a field of freshly mown hay, between a white Rolls-Royce and a Rover. Tables set with white linen on the paved patio outside the west front of the church enticed me into the sloping churchyard.

The man who was then rector but has since retired, the Rev. Rex Hancock, was leaning on the front gate, with a beaming, rosy-faced smile of welcome. Church bells pealed out in a charmingly eccentric fashion, the result of three people attempting to ring four of the six available, with one woman ringing two at once.

This church in West Quantoxhead, Somerset, is dedicated to the virgin St Etheldreda, commonly called St Audry, Queen of Northumbria. She became first Abbess of Ely and died in AD 679 of a throat tumour, which she considered a punishment for wearing necklaces in her youth.

This is the biggest of seven churches in the combined benefice, now in the care of the Rev. Andrew Stevens. In some rural parts of England, one clergyman or woman can be in charge of as many as ten churches. Most of Mr Stevens' churches have congregations of ten to fifteen, but for our service there were about thirty.

Inside, the worshippers seemed to fill the few rows of gleaming pews, which can hold about 200. The red-tiled polished floor, carved pulpit and choir stalls were set off by a riotous display of golden chrysanthemums, lilies, gladioli and alstroemeria, pink delphiniums, red anthurium, cream carnations, preserved mahonia and other exotic flora, complemented by the flowery dresses worn by nearly every woman present.

The choir of eight women and three men processed up the aisle to the introit, an organ rendition of 'All Things Bright and Beautiful', the theme of that week's flower festival. As we launched into the first hymn, the sensation of being in the archetypal country parish church was augmented by the apparent inability of some members of the congregation to sing in tune.

Aided by the lusty voices of the choir, which drowned out our faulty notes, we sang popular hymns to folk melodies, such as 'Sent forth by God's blessing' to the tune of 'The Ash Grove'. We proceeded at a brisk pace through the communion service, set out in the Church of England Alternative Service Book. Hymn, confession, readings, sermon and the Creed came to their conclusion in the sacrament of Holy Communion, well within the allotted hour preferred by most Anglicans.

Mr Hancock is a former master of beagles, fishes regularly and used to ride to hounds. He joined forces with a parishioner, Capt. Tony Bailey, a former naval skipper, to create his own polo team, the Kilve Kippers. Parishioners still speak of the day they beat the Weston-super-Mare B side.

Mr Hancock decided to become a clergyman after a dramatic conversion at a Billy Graham rally in north London in 1954. He spent twenty years as an army padre with the cavalry. Vestiges of the pre-Christian Mr Hancock remain, however. He was called up before Dr George Carey, now Archbishop of Canterbury but then Bishop of Bath and Wells, after he used 'unparliamentary' language to a journalist.

His sermon, a considered piece of plain speaking, was delivered with classic, Anglican-style intonations. 'Be prepared' is the motto of the Scout movement, he said. 'It is not only boy scouts, but all Christian people who should have this as their motto today. Be prepared, be on your watch, be on your guard. Repent and be baptised.' In few places are church politics more impassioned than at parish level.

After the service, some members of the congregation, with a

sense of quiet importance, conveyed information to me of varying degrees of intrigue. A relative-by-marriage of the Archdeacon of London, the Ven. George Cassidy, pleaded his case that St Ethelburga's, destroyed by the IRA bomb in the City, should not be rebuilt. Local dignitaries were offended by the size of the parish 'quota', the fixed contribution each church pays towards its priest's stipend, perceived and resented as a goad to giving. A farmer, Duncan Stafford, was investigating the parish records, which go back to 1559, to discover the fate of a baby boy abandoned in the eighteenth century.

There was talk of how the Bishop of Bath and Wells, the Right Rev. Jim Thompson, had bought a horse, was learning to ride and planned to preach on horseback at Mr Hancock's 'animals' service' at nearby Plud Farm, Stringston. There was the necessary introduction to Effie, the rector's old grey mare, in a nearby field.

The congregation represented more than 10 per cent of the population of the parish. When we took tea outside, and visitors began to crowd into the church to look at the flowers, I asked about the boarded-up building opposite. It turned out to have been a public house, closed down while the church has continued to thrive. This was a curious reversal of the perceived trend of church decline elsewhere. The service suggested that claims by the Church of England that the decline has bottomed out and signs of growth are beginning could be believed.

SERVICES: telephone for details.

Five Cathedrals Tour with the Classic and Historic
Motor Club
Guildford Cathedral
(Tel: 01483 65287)
Wells Cathedral
WELLS
(Tel: 01749 674483)

DEAN OF GUILDFORD: The Very Rev. Alexander Wedderspoon.

DEAN OF WELLS: The Very Rev. Richard Lewis.

ARCHITECTURE: Improved immeasurably as we journeyed south-west from Guildford to Wells, from new to old.

SERMON: None at evensong at Wells.

MUSIC: Deep, languorous tones of Rolls-Royce horn accompanied our journey. At evensong, the Wells cathedral voluntary choir sang Purcell's 'O God the King of Glory' and Ayleward responses. The cathedral choir, famous worldwide for its singing, was off duty because it had just completed a long service for the ordination of women priests.

LITURGY: From the 1662 Book of Common Prayer.

AFTER-SERVICE CARE: Tea and scones with the Mayor of Wells, Kate Fry, before evensong, followed by thrilling high-speed ride in beltless 1962 duck-egg blue Sunbeam Rapier on a country road to Bath to catch the 19.27 to London.

SPIRITUAL HIGH: A moving and emotive experience, in a Rolls with an engine so smooth I could hear the clock ticking as if to eternity.

With the peal of Maximus on twelve bells ringing in our ears, we left the austere, somewhat forbidding Guildford Cathedral in a 1936 fixed phaeton 25/30 Rolls-Royce. Behind us, a bright red Sunbeam Alpine stole some of the glances of amazed pedestrians.

We and about twenty other old cars were heading for Wells Cathedral in Somerset.

Similar processions were making their way from Exeter, Bristol and Coventry, to meet up in time for evensong at Wells, the smallest city in England, where Bishop Jim Thompson was that day ordaining fifteen women priests. This was the first cathedrals tour organised by the Classic and Historic Motor Club, a curious amalgam of the sacred and secular that seemed entirely appropriate once the various drivers had explained to me how like a religion their hobby had become to them.

Classic car enthusiast Trish Burridge, wife of Gerald, owner of the Rolls and other classics, said: 'It is an appreciation of old things. I like old buildings, old furniture, old houses.' Most of the drivers, in common with many churchgoers, were on the older side, and dressed in smart but English understated Sunday best. 'There are those who take it to tremendous extremes,' added Trish, who is on the flower rota of her parish church at Ston Easton, Somerset and who is embroidering a new frontal for the altar.

We sped along in the comfort of leather seats with arm rests but without the luxury of heating or a car stereo. She continued: 'You could say some of them worship their cars. They will drive round puddles rather than go through them.' At a pit stop at Fairleigh Hungerford Castle near Bath in Wiltshire, with its fourteenth-century chapel, we met company director Guy Bromley, anxious that his 1954 red MG TF, with only 58,000 miles on the clock, was doomed shortly to be soaked by rain. Such an event, he confirmed, came close to being a spiritual experience. The exhilaration of driving a car such as his to intimate proximity with a cathedral such as Wells made even getting the car wet worthwhile.

The drive from the massive, hilltop gaucheness of Guildford Cathedral, with its beautifully light limestone interior, completed in 1961, to the intricate and Gothic splendour of fourteenth and fifteenth century Wells, a true journey from the sacred to the divine, was completed in about four hours.

Evensong in the twelfth- and thirteenth-century quire of Wells awaited us, a warm and inviting sanctuary from the hostile wind and rain outside. I sat in front of the Dean of Wells, the Very Rev. Richard Lewis, in what would normally be his wife's stall and opposite the precentor, Canon Paul Lucas. As the choir sang the 'Nunc Dimittis', the Song of Simeon, 'Lord now lettest thou thy servant depart in peace, according to thy word' echoed softly around the tracery.

'Lighten our darkness, we beseech thee O Lord; and by thy great mercy defend us from all perils and dangers of this night,' intoned Marcus Laing, vicar choral, as he sent us off into the darkening evening.

Outside, the great headlamps of the assembled cars lit up one by one, and we glided off smoothly from the cathedral lawn and through the narrow streets of Wells, to face once more the shadows of the open road.

Contact: Bill Willcocks, Thomas St, Wells, Somerset BA5 2UY (01749 675486).

St Basil and All Saints
Hough Green Road
WIDNES
Cheshire
(Roman Catholic Tel: 0151–424 6641
Church of England Tel: 0151–420 4963)

PARISH PRIEST: Father Peter McGrail.
VICAR: The Rev. Ray Bridson.
ARCHITECTURE: Dark purple brick outside with golden brick
  inside to match the beech fittings.
SERMON: None, but useful debate with two clergy at the end of
  the service on the 'marriage' of their two churches.
MUSIC: None at this service; usually there is an organ or folk
  group, with guitarists, flutes, recorders, clarinets and percussion.
LITURGY: Divine office from the Roman Catholic breviary for
  a shared Catholic and Anglican service.
AFTER-SERVICE CARE: Tea, coffee and sometimes wine after
  9.45 a.m.
SPIRITUAL HIGH: Strangely moving, considering the brevity of
  the service.

St Basil and All Saints at Widnes, in Cheshire, is one of the few
combined Anglican and Catholic churches in Britain. The vicarage
and presbytery stand on either side of the church, which was built
in the early 1980s to serve the new Upton and Cherry Sutton
housing estates. Many came to the parish from the Dingle and
Speke areas of Liverpool, where strong sectarian rivalries existed
between Protestants and Catholics.

On one wall of the church there is a striking bronze sculpture
depicting St Basil the Great, surrounded by modern figures, such as
Dietrich Bonhoeffer, who tried to assassinate Hitler. The Rev. Ray
Bridson, the Anglican vicar who is called 'Father' by parishioners,
said: 'Those shown with St Basil are contemporary or recent figures
whose lives and actions convey what we feel to be the essence of
sainthood and Christian values. The idea was that holy men and
women are not just people in stained-glass windows.' About 400
people attend the Catholic mass on Sunday and 100 the Anglican

eucharist. I went to the shared service, evening prayer or vespers, which was unrepresentative in terms of numbers, but gave a sense of the spirit of ecumenism because, although we used the Catholic rite, the service was taken by the Anglican vicar.

It appeared that vespers has still to catch on in the wider church. Terri Cloherty, the mother of four children and chair of the parent-teacher association of St Basil's primary school, was the only congregant, apart from myself and the photographer.

We said evening prayer from the Catholic Divine Office, the 'liturgy of the hours', which sets out worship of God throughout the day. The office followed the classic pattern of Christian worship: a reading, a response and a prayer. We sat in the second pew with Father Paul Crowe, who was then the Roman Catholic parish priest, who guided us through the book, while Fr Bridson led the service, seated on the front pew. We did not sing but said the hymn, 'Praise to the Holiest in the Height', by John Henry Newman, which seemed appropriate: Newman founded the high church Oxford Movement in the Church of England before joining the Catholic church and becoming a cardinal. The entire service lasted about ten minutes.

The church was built with a vestry and the Catholic equivalent, a sacristy, but now the two clergy share the sacristy and the vestry has been turned into a resource room with overhead projectors, videos and tapes, where they hold joint classes to prepare people for adult baptism and confirmation.

Initially, the Catholics worshipped in a dual-purpose church hall, and the Anglicans met in their own school hall. A decade later, both needed new church buildings and opted to build one and share it. The foundation stone was blessed by Pope John Paul II on his visit to the UK in 1982, and the church was completed the following year.

There are a few indications that this is not an ordinary church. A holy water stoop on the left of the entrance porch is used by Catholics and a few Anglicans to make the sign of the cross as they enter the church. Members of both denominations light the votive candles and say prayers beneath the statue of the Virgin Mary on the east side. Piles of blue Anglican service books and brown Catholic missals are piled side by side.

The beech pews form a semi-circle around the one altar and a crucifix donated by the Roman Catholic Archbishop of Liverpool, the Most Rev. Derek Worlock, and the Anglican bishop, the Right Rev. David Sheppard. The font combines the old oak and modern brass of those used by the churches when they met separately.

On important holy days, the two congregations take part in 'sim-ultaneous celebrations of the eucharist'. Anglicans and Catholics are told clearly to go to their own clergy to receive communion.

According to the two clergy, the visibility of their unity has discomfited some in both dioceses. The debate has reached even the ears of the Vatican.

At times, concern has been expressed over the practice of holding joint eucharists and of keeping the 'reserved sacrament' of both denominations in the one tabernacle, a brass receptacle on the sanctuary wall. Reserved sacrament consists of a small amount of the elements kept back after mass or eucharist for visits to the sick or housebound. A red light on the wall burns when the sacrament is present.

Although the two sacraments at Widnes are kept in separate compartments, and both clergy trust each other not to touch or use the wrong one, critics fear tampering could take place. I asked Fr Crowe whether he considered Fr Bridson's orders to be valid. He answered: 'If someone said to me, "Is Ray a priest?" I would say, yes of course, he is in the Church of England.' Everything they do is within the strictures of a closely worded legal document, which sets out the rules for their shared arrangements. Mrs Cloherty, a member of the joint church council which meets bi-monthly to co-ordinate adminstration, maintenance and some pastoral work, said: 'It works well. When we have a joint service, you would not know who was Catholic and who was Church of England. Everyone is ecumenical. There is no selfishness.' Fr Crowe said: 'We let the theologians have the theological debates. At the end of the day we are working for one church, united in heart, mind, belief and love.'

SERVICES: mass 8.30 a.m. and 11.15 a.m.; Anglican parish eucharist 9.45 a.m.; shared evening prayer 6 p.m.

The Queen's Free Chapel of St George within Her Castle of Windsor
Windsor Castle
WINDSOR
Berkshire SL4 1NJ
(Tel: 01753 865538)

DEAN: The Very Rev. Patrick Mitchell.

ARCHITECTURE: Built in the late fifteen- and early sixteenth-century perpendicular style, the chapel reflects the splendour of a French Gothic cathedral, but with the intimacy of an English parish church.

SERMON: The dean preached on baptism and on the mark of a saint, a 'strange blend of humility, sorrow and joy'. Uplifting and amusing.

MUSIC: The choir, famous worldwide, dates from 1352. Of more than 70 boys in the choir school, twenty-four are choristers. The choir includes twelve men, or lay clerks, who live in the castle as members of St George's college. The non-religious as well as the religious should go, simply to hear them sing.

LITURGY: We used the more traditional of the modern service rites. Plush cushions made kneeling a pleasurable respite.

AFTER-SERVICE CARE: Friendly chat with dean and canons, with chance to take tea at one of many nearby cafes in the town centre at the foot of Windsor castle. Royal watchers who go to the Queen's Free Chapel of St George to see the Queen at church on Sunday are likely to be disappointed. The Queen, castle staff and Crown employees who live in Windsor Great Park usually attend her own private chapel within the grounds of the Royal Lodge in Windsor Great Park.

SPIRITUAL HIGH: The discovery that an idealised spiritual fantasy actually exists.

The Queen and her family do go to St George's on Easter Day and other formal occasions, when the public is welcome. But St George's is well worth a visit in its own right, simply to marvel at the exquisite music and architecture.

The chapel is free in the sense that it is not under the jurisdiction of a bishop or archbishop. It is the spiritual home of the Most

Noble Order of the Garter, and the quire has possibly the finest display of historic heraldry in the world. Seated before us in statuesque splendour in the lower stalls were the Military Knights of Windsor, originally called the poor or alms knights, in decorative scarlet uniforms last redesigned in the time of William IV. Technically these are deputies of the Knights of the Garter. All are distinguished soldiers, a general, brigadiers, colonels and majors who live within the castle walls.

The Most Noble Order of the Garter, the oldest existing monarchical order of chivalry, was founded by Edward III in 1348 after the capture of Calais. Besides a banner, helm with a crest sword and mantling, every knight has a brass stall plate, and this is the only heraldic achievement which remains in place in the quire after death. All other items are removed, to be replaced by those of his successor. The oldest of the 750 brass and enamel plates is that of Lord Basset, which dates from about 1390.

St George's feels like the ultimate parish church, where pre- and post-Reformation history intermingle in colourful and at times bewildering display. Those of us who stayed after matins for communion walked to the rail over a stone marking the burial vault of Charles I, Henry VIII and Henry's third wife, Jane Seymour, who died giving birth. In front of us, the grey morning light filtered through the nineteenth-century Clayton and Bell stained-glass in the east window, showing the magnificent fifteenth century William Berkeley woodwork at its best. And in the unlikely event of the view from the pew becoming dull, we could browse through an impressive display of service books.

Because it was matins, a choir office, the clergy wore choir habit, with murrey, or mulberry, cassocks and surplice, scarf and hood. For communion they changed into white and gold copes with stoles. The friendliness of the clergy, combined with the impressive surroundings, made visitors feel welcome but also rather privileged to be there at all.

Matins, or morning prayer as it is sometimes called, grew out of the monastic tradition, when monks divided the day into 'hours' of prayer. Since the Reformation, it has been associated mainly with the Church of England. Recently, a few Roman Catholic churches have started to celebrate morning prayer with their congregations, although it has always been part of worship in monasteries and convents. We began with a prayer, confession, a hymn and a psalm, followed by the first lesson, a canticle, the second lesson and another hymn. The most beautiful part was the intercessory prayers, when the dean recited his own compilation, beginning with prayers for the Queen and for the Most Noble Order of the Garter. We prayed that Christians everywhere, mindful of baptism, might witness eternal values and truth, that we might so pass through things temporal, that we find and not lose the things eternal.

This was followed by a rare event, the publication of banns of marriage between Gary Wilson, a bachelor of Windsor Castle, and Christine Ansell of Windsor. St George's, a self-governing secular community of priests, laymen and women, has no parish and weddings are infrequent. Mr Wilson is the son of Fred Wilson, the castle's clerk of works.

The dean took his text from St Paul's letter to the Colossians. He described how, walking the dogs that morning in Windsor Great Park, he encountered a jogger in a sweater bearing the message 'Saints'. The dean stopped the startled runner to ask him if he was called to be a saint. The man replied: 'Oh no, I am only a saint in the football sense.' The dean continued. 'Now, who actually wants to be a saint in the Christian sense in England these days? It is not a popular notion. But we are called to be holy, and that is something exciting, as he who calls us is holy.' He preached about baptism. 'June 10, 1930, was a great date for me,' he stated. 'It was the date of my baptism in the parish church of St Andrew, Whitestaunton, Somerset. Do you all know the date of your baptism? If not, find out. It should be a great day of thanksgiving, a day to receive Holy Communion in thanksgiving. Your baptism and my baptism are the foundation on which to build our Christian life. From our baptism, the call to us from God is the call to be saints.' The chapel supports a study centre, St George's House, founded in 1966, which holds regular courses and meetings to examine contemporary issues.

Nearly all the income to support the chapel comes from donations. All collections are given away, ours went to Christian Aid. The Friends of St George's pay for big structural repairs. The chapel might have fabulous spiritual wealth, but, like so many Anglican churches, it labours under a myth of great material wealth. Its annual income some years was only just enough to make ends meet.

All who wish can attend the four Sunday services and nineteenth regular weekday services.

SUNDAY SERVICES: Holy Communion 8.30 a.m.; matins 10.45 a.m.; sung eucharist 11.45 a.m.; evensong 5.15 p.m.

The Church of England Parish of St Luke's
Burton Stone Lane
YORK
(Tel: 01904 634145)

VICAR: The Rev. John McGrath.

NON-STIPENDIARY MINISTER: The Rev. Bill Ankers.

ARCHITECTURE: Built early this century, but the money ran out after the nave was finished and the aisles were never built. Bright and cheery effect achieved by red carpet and white walls.

SERMON: The controversial Ven. George Austin, Archdeacon of York, was refreshingly spiritual and amusing.

MUSIC: Small choir of boys and girls in blue robes led us in songs from the evangelical hymn book *Mission Praise*. A group played during communion.

LITURGY: Rite A of the Anglican Alternative Service Book.

AFTER-SERVICE CARE: Excellent coffee, tea, biscuits and a friendly chat.

SPIRITUAL HIGH: The warmth of the congregation wholly offset the sadness of the incomplete building in a poor area.

'Good morning, the Archdemon has arrived,' the Rev. Bill Ankers announced as I walked into the red-brick church of St Luke's. He was referring to the Archdeacon of York, the Ven. George Austin, that day's guest preacher. Mr Austin was likened by his own Archbishop, Dr John Habgood, to Charles Dickens' Fat Boy in *The Pickwick Papers*. He received hate mail after he condemned the Prince of Wales's alleged relationship with Camilla Parker Bowles. But his reception at St Luke's showed him to be a man in touch with middle England and middle-of-the-road Anglicanism.

Mr Ankers belongs to the expanding ranks of non-stipendiary ministers in the Church of England. These are men and women, often with full-time secular jobs, who can find themselves doing a 24-hour-a-day ministry as well. Mr Ankers explained that they can be 'prophets to the church as to what actually happens within the world' as well as witness as Christians in their secular workplace and sometimes work also as an unpaid assistant curate for their local church. When a parish like St Luke's is between vicars, as it was when I visited, non-stipendiary ministers such as Mr Ankers become indispensable.

Mr Ankers's secular work is as a car dealer, so it was no surprise when he asked for a moment's silence 'to still the traffic in our busy lives'. The Bible readings were dramatic. From Numbers 15, we heard the story of a man stoned to death for gathering firewood on the Sabbath, and from John's Gospel that of the woman caught in the act of adultery.

Then Mr Austin began to preach on the love of God and on the need for self-examination during Lent. He referred to boring church services, dull sermons and an insomniac he knew 'who for twenty years loved coming to church because it was the only time he could sleep'.

Our prayers were led by a member of the congregation, a former Baptist, before we moved into the confession and the peace, when the clergy joined us in the nave as we all shook hands.

In its eclecticism, St Luke's felt like a microcosm of the Church of England as it is today. Bells were rung and incense issued forth during the eucharistic prayers, but we had fresh, leavened bread instead of the unleavened hosts for communion, and an evangelical-style group with guitar and electric piano sang as we walked to and from the altar rail. The final words from Mr Austin were characteristically dramatic: 'I take no pleasure in anyone's death, says the Lord. Repent and Live.'

Over coffee, a former Roman Catholic explained why St Luke's had tempted him into Anglicanism. Jim Harland, a regular member since 1977 when he helped fix the organ, said: 'It was the warmth of the people who greeted me.' He is now a churchwarden. Mr Harland said: 'We sometimes have to put extra seating out because so many people come.'

SUNDAY SERVICES: communion 9.30 a.m.; evening prayer 6.30 p.m.

Index